# Lateral Thinking Disruptive Creativity

\-

## Live your dreams

MICHAEL MUXWORTHY

# DEDICATION

To the many hundreds of lateral thinking enthusiasts who regularly interact with me via my author website, michaelmuxworthy.com. I love our debates, your amazing insights, and your invaluable contributions. Much of the evolutionary thinking that appears within these pages is a direct consequence of our interactions. Thank you so much. This book is dedicated to you.

*'Life's great purpose is to evolve.*

*'It is our capacity for creativity that makes human evolution so exceptional.'*

\- Michael Muxworthy

# CONTENTS

**Introduction**                                                                1

**Chapter One – Understand**                                                     4

- What *exactly* is lateral thinking?
- Blinkered thinking
- Random starting points (RSPs)
- Lateral thinking puzzles
- The relationship with humor

**Chapter Two – Develop skills**                                                 16

- Alternative perspective
- Provocative operation, or 'po'
- Puzzle break – Their last dance
- Backwards planning
- Competition Vs differentiation
- Teach as you learn
- Teach as you learn – Every character has a story to tell
- Puzzle break – That sinking feeling
- Question existing patterns
- Are you keeping up?

**Chapter Three – Build proficiency**                                            34

- Practice exercise – A new small business venture
- Puzzle break – Jealousy
- 'Exceptional' goal setting
- Teach as you learn – Random games, activities, & inputs
- Puzzle break – What happened to Betty?
- Teach as you learn – Planning backwards

## Chapter Four – Expand your skills 51

- Creative combinations
- Challenge dominant thinking
- Public speaking
- Puzzle break – Angry shark
- Random starting points - Word association extension
- Practice exercise – The new marina

## Chapter Five – Take the lead 68

- Six thinking hats
- Puzzle break – The helpful barman
- Quick review
- Teach as you learn – Question existing patterns
- Time management
- Puzzle break – Easily recognized
- Problem solving

## Chapter Six – The big picture 87

- Patterns that disrupt
- Teach as you learn – The lost art of conversation
- Pulling it all together
- Puzzle break – Itchy trigger finger

## A final word 97

## Glossary of terms and original definitions 100

## Notable Muxy quotes 102

MICHAEL MUXWORTHY

# Introduction

I recently faced a confrontational situation while waiting in line to order coffee at my favorite local café. The exchange *shattered* rigid beliefs I've held for a very long time. It is a powerful example of lateral thinking in action. Let me share what happened …

At a table in the back of the café sat an old and fragile-looking gentleman who was on the receiving end of a lecture from an educated-sounding young man passionate about his atheist beliefs—too passionate perhaps. It was impossible not to overhear their 'conversation'. Despite his fragility, the old guy wasn't backing down.

"There's no such thing as God!" the young man said too loudly. "God didn't just magically appear and create everything. We've evolved over millions of years. Evolution is real!"

Several customers left without purchasing.

"Evolution is just a theory. Science is always getting things wrong," the old man countered. He looked and sounded distressed. "They'll come up with something entirely different in a few years. You'll see."

The café's owner, whom I know very well, caught my eye, looked towards the rowdy table, and returned to me with a smile.

(Okay, can you picture this scene? Imagine you're there with me. Let's continue ...)

I approached the table in a non-threatening way and politely introduced myself, deciding to stay only long enough to be sure that the old man would be okay. It turned out the pair were related. The young man was his grandson.

"How do *you* explain evolution?" the young man asked of me.

I've always held very strong views about religion and evolution that fall heavily on one side of this argument. Which side? It makes no difference. The point is that the viewpoints seem irreconcilable. My initial instinct was to limit my involvement to quietening the debate, but I couldn't resist the old man's pleading eyes.

"Try to answer the question of evolution from an 'alternative perspective'—God's perspective," I said.

"There's no such thing as God," the grandson insisted.

"But you can imagine that God exists, and you can imagine how He might answer that question if evolution really does exist," I said. "For the moment, imagine YOU are God, and that evolution is real. Are you both in the role?"

"Yes," they both answered almost simultaneously.

"How do *you* explain evolution?"

To their tremendous credit, they both thought seriously about the question from the imagined perspective of God.

"I suppose evolution could exist if God made it so," conceded the old man.

"Evolution isn't necessarily the defining proof that there is no God that I'd always assumed," conceded the grandson.

I had *not* seen that coming. My views were 'blinkered' also.

It didn't settle the argument one way or the other, but both sides of the argument gained something new. 'Alternative perspective' is just one of many simple, disruptive lateral thinking strategies I hope you'll adopt throughout these pages.

*'If science and religion BOTH genuinely seek the truth, eventually they MUST agree.'*

(If you'd like to comment on this example, or on any of the examples, definitions, exercises, quotations, and theories that appear within these pages, your feedback, alternative views, and criticisms are *all* most welcome. Join the community. Please submit via the 'Contact' page on my author website: michaelmuxworthy.com. N.B. Comments and/or contributions that are submitted may be published on my websites without seeking permission or giving notice).

# Chapter One - Understand

## What *exactly* is 'lateral thinking'?

The term 'lateral thinking' was first coined by Edward de Bono as an all-encompassing 'label' for disruptive processes that are used to facilitate and inspire creative thinking. De Bono's intended meaning of the term has been lost and confused over time and should *not* be equated with literal interpretations.

There are far too many definitions of lateral thinking 'out there'. They're often overly complex, or singularly focused on 'problem solving'. They are *all* inadequate to the task. Here's my own take that is simple, comprehensive, *and* fits with de Bono's original intentions. Definition:

*'Lateral thinking is a deliberate process of disrupting existing patterns so that new and original ways of combining things can be revealed.'*

It's really that simple. In the above example, we took 'evolution is real' and 'God exists', and we used an imagined 'alternative perspective' as a tool to disrupt rigid mindsets (patterns) for the purpose of searching for an original way to combine them. I do this sort of stuff all the time. It comes naturally to me, and soon it will for you too.

Consider the broad category of creativity. Definition:

*'Creativity is the combining of existing things in new and original ways.'*

The artist painting a masterpiece combines existing colors, materials, skills, and thoughts in a new way. A good novelist is merely combining letters, words, and themes in new ways. That latest hit on the radio you can't get out of your head is a combination of notes, instruments, and technologies that already exist. The award-winning architect combines technologies, designs, shapes, and materials … you get the idea.

For most of us, these types of creativity can only be admired as there are intangible qualities (or gifts) involved that are out of our reach. Unlike all other forms of creativity though, creative thinking is something that is within reach of everyone. Definition:

*'Creative thinking is the ability to imagine existing things in new and original combinations.'*

When Wilber and Orville Wright created the first successful powered airplane, it was a creative thinking journey that had started in their imaginations. They imagined themselves being able to fly by combining things that already existed such as the aerodynamics of birds for flight, an engine for propulsion, materials to construct the frame, and engineering to somehow hold it all together.

Lateral thinking unleashes your creative thinking potential. As you learn and practice the simple skills revealed within these pages, new patterns (neural pathways) of good creative habits will embed themselves within your psyche. You *will* become an accomplished and consistent creative thinker by the time you finish reading this book.

Lateral thinking is a simple, fast, and proven pathway to creative thinking.

(What do you think about my original definitions? I *welcome* your views and thoughts via: michaelmuxworthy.com)

## Blinkered thinking

We start life with unfettered imaginations. The combinations that come from children are fun, uplifting, and creative. They're natural creative thinkers.

As we advance through life, we adopt patterns (habits/neural pathways/memories/expertise) that 'shackle' us to preconceived ideas, social norms/groups, our education, and our personal experiences. We find comfort, safety, efficiency, and simplicity by repeating patterns of learned behavior, rather than constantly seeking out new ways or 'starting from scratch', and that's okay. It would be enormously inefficient, for example, if we had to learn to drive every time we needed to hop into the car. However, patterns of learned behavior inhibit our capacity for creative thinking, as the following puzzle demonstrates.

Try solving this …

Instructions:

- Use three separate lines (straight or curved) to join the boxes labeled with letters. Use a single line to join 'A' to 'A', 'B' to 'B', and 'C' to 'C'.
- The lines cannot touch or cross each other.
- The lines must stay inside the black lines of the diagram and cannot touch the sides.
- The lines cannot touch or go through other boxes.

There is no trick involved.

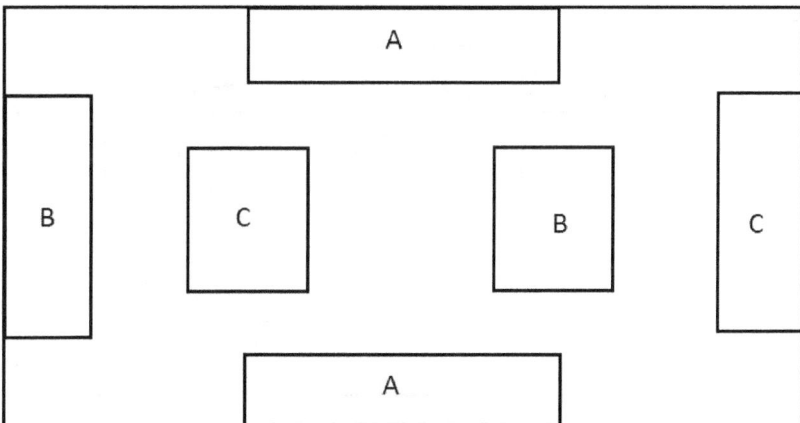

Having trouble? Here's a clue ...

You likely can't solve the problem because of your expertise. You know two things:

- 'A' comes before 'B' and 'C', and
- The shortest distance between two points is a straight line.

Okay, so you likely imagined a straight line from 'A' to 'A' and immediately ruled it out as it makes joining the 'B' and 'C' boxes impossible. Next, logically, you diverted the 'A' to 'A' line around 'B' or 'C' to no avail. Most people stop at this point believing there's some sort of 'trick' involved. Your expertise is working against you.

Try giving this puzzle to a young child that doesn't have such rigid patterns in place. They'll often join the 'B' or 'C' boxes first and the solution appears effortlessly. You'll be surprised how often they'll solve the puzzle almost immediately.

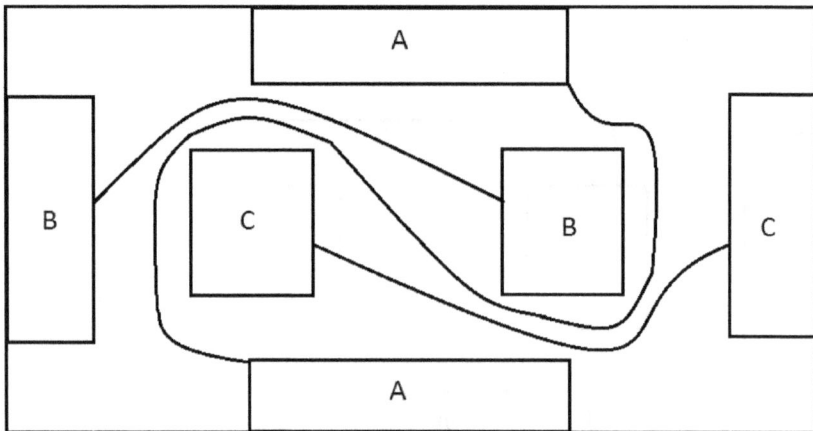

The solution seems obvious … *now.*

Think about the number of traffic lights and dangerous intersections we face unnecessarily because of the decisions made by 'blinkered' town planners who immediately connect 'A' to 'A' with a straight road and congratulate themselves on their expertise, ha, ha.

So many things in life are exactly like this puzzle. There are solutions and/or superior alternatives open to us, if only we could see them. With so many existing successful patterns (or 'off-the-shelf' solutions) available to us, our 'need' to innovate diminishes.

Let's look at your first very simple lateral thinking disruption strategy to understand how easy it is to generate creative thinking ...

## Random starting points (RSPs)

*Family (dis)harmony.*

Several years ago, I pulled our household (myself, my partner, and her two teenage daughters) together to try to decide on where to go for the summer holidays. Weeks had passed without resolution as each person had a preconceived 'best' holiday agenda—me included. To break through the impasse, I generated an RSP.

Pinning a map of Australia to the wall, I gave a throwing dart to my lovely (but slightly inebriated at the time) partner, suggesting that we think about what we could do in or around wherever the dart landed. Well, she threw the dart, and despite being close and the map being of considerable size, she missed completely.

A boat!

I contacted a good friend who agreed to let me borrow his 'family friendly' sailboat to explore some of Australia's southeast coast. Each member of the family was allowed to choose two destinations and/or experiences along the way. It was hugely successful, and in hindsight, the solution seemed obvious.

So, what happened here? We took existing 'things', and we combined them in a new and original way (at least for us). A disruptive input (the RSP) broke the shackles of our rigid mindsets to reveal an escape pathway. Let's work through a lateral thinking RSP exercise …

Your mission: Reduce the road toll, carbon emissions, and average vehicle travel times with ONE simple innovation.

Let's generate our first RSP. I've picked up a book, opened it at a random page, and selected a keyword from the second paragraph— 'magnet'. How could a magnet achieve these objectives?

Okay, some of the ideas I came up with were:

- Magnets on the front and back of vehicles to connect them on highways to slip stream efficiently and safely.
- Magnetic swipe cards or barcodes on vehicles that identify vehicles at checkpoints, record their journey, and determine whether they travel at safe speeds, rest regularly on long journeys, and generally operate in an efficient manner.
- Magnetic field sensors that detect engine activity at traffic lights could be positioned well before intersections to 'anticipate' traffic demand and compute more efficient outcomes.

And I have it! My idea— 'smart intersections'. Instead of traffic lights changing at regular predetermined intervals, the intersection is 'informed' of all traffic (and the specifications of different vehicles) approaching from all directions enabling it to determine safe and efficient solutions. I'm sure the technology is within easy reach.

You'll note that my final solution has nothing to do with magnets. The

RSP 'magnet' was simply a way to break free of familiar thinking to instead stimulate new and/or original combinations. RSPs can be as simple as a random word or number, the first thing you see, a random suggestion from someone ... I'm sure you get the idea.

Lateral thinking doesn't guarantee to deliver solutions or productive outcomes, but it does promise new and original combinations regularly and reliably. More than often, it will deliver viable alternatives, and sometimes it delivers truly remarkable results. The RSP disruptions demonstrated above I would describe as 'shotgun' type approaches. We'll be learning about more 'targeted' methods soon.

## Lateral thinking puzzles

Lateral thinking puzzles are situation puzzles that require explanation. They have multiple answers that aren't necessarily right or wrong; instead, they're subjectively judged on the plausibility of their explanation. For example ...

*Snoring Sam ... ZZZ.*

The sound of Sam's snoring is normally just annoying, but today it causes terror and panic. Why?

Answer one: Sam is a bus driver. His passengers hear his snoring and panic.

Answer two: Sam is an emergency call telephone operator. A killer is trying to break down your door.

Answer three: Sam is a commercial airline pilot reporting a strange 'smell' to Air Traffic Control.

Lateral thinking puzzles are a great way to refresh creativity and lift the energy at meetings, in classrooms, or even during lectures, and I'll be using them occasionally throughout these pages to maintain your focus. Lateral thinking puzzles are always fun and uplifting because they involve humor. Lateral thinking's relationship with humor is an important one …

## The relationship with humor

Maltese psychologist Dr. Edward de Bono considered humor (such as a joke) to be 'like' lateral thinking in that it involves an 'insight switchover' from a familiar pattern to something new and/or unexpected—a pattern-switching process. Jokes trigger laughter because they reveal combinations that make sense in unexpected ways. Lateral thinking disrupts familiar patterns so that creative thinking can explore combinations (solutions/opportunities) that make sense in unexpected ways.

*'Humor is the most significant behavior of the human mind.'*

- Dr. Edward de Bono

Lateral thinking and humor are both 'sideways' thinking in that they reveal alternative pathways not in your immediate focus.

**Alternative, or** **'escape' pathways**

**Dominant thinking >>>**

Joke: Why do we tell actors to 'break a leg'?

Dominant thinking sends us down the path of 'to wish them luck'. However, when I reveal an unexpected alternative or 'escape' pathway that has always been there but not immediately apparent, the unexpected answer is seen as humor.

Unexpected answer or solution: Because every play needs a cast. (We combined an alternative meaning of 'cast' to 'break a leg'.)

Definition:

> *'Dominant thinking is a prevailing pattern recognized as being established, successful, or a logical way forward.'*

Now let's look at a complex problem with a dominant thinking way forward, and an unexpected solution …

*At risk teen.*

Problem: A regular visitor to my author website told me that her teenage daughter was terrified of being 'judged' and therefore had trouble being around, communicating with, and meeting new people. She'd dropped out of school, had no friends, seemed angry all the time, and rarely ventured outside. Her only contact with the outside world were people she interacted with online.

Dominant thinking leads us down the path of counseling and professional help—something the daughter refused absolutely. We have a dominant thinking impasse.

Lateral thinking disruption: Consider the 'alternative perspective' of one of the daughter's online contacts. 'How is it that she's okay interacting with you online?'

The online person's response: 'Maybe it's because she can remain anonymous. I don't really know who she is. She never shows her real face.' (Hmmm, our thinking has been disrupted away from professional help).

Unexpected creative thinking solution to the problem: Dress up in costume when she leaves home to remain anonymous. Any time she feels 'recognized', change her costume and appearance completely.

True story. The daughter started by dressing up for special events such as Comic-Con and concerts, and within months she'd made a friend and felt confident enough to begin slowly and gradually removing the layers of her various 'disguises'.

Was it the best solution? I have no idea as I'm not an expert. My point is that, just like humor, the unexpected alternative always existed. We just had to find a way to reveal it—to unleash our creative thinking. That is lateral thinking's purpose.

Next, let's take a deeper dive into 'alternative perspective', a powerful and 'targeted' lateral thinking disruption strategy for initiating creative thinking …

(You can submit your own lateral thinking puzzles, or examples of lateral thinking in real-life action, via the 'Contact' page on my author website: michaelmuxworthy.com. Top contributions will be published on my websites, with full credit given to contributors).

# Chapter Two – Develop skills

## Alternative perspective

In the introduction, we considered the imagined 'alternative perspective' of God during an argument at my local café. We didn't settle the argument, but we *did* generate an interesting combination to challenge rigid beliefs that brought the temperature down, and the opposing sides closer. *Remember, lateral thinking doesn't guarantee solutions or outcomes. It is merely a tool—a very powerful tool.* Like most tools, you'll get better results with practice. Let's work through a simple exercise …

*Where there's smoke, there's fire.*

You are a senior detective who has been sent to investigate a warehouse fire in an isolated area. An experienced police officer, who arrived at the scene earlier, informs you that the rear door had been forced, the safe inside cut open, and that the distraught business owner told him that there'd been a lot of cash in the safe. The officer said that he'd smelled the fumes of some sort of fire accelerant when he'd first arrived. The officer speculates that one or more burglars forced their way into the premises, robbed the safe, and lit a fire afterwards to destroy any evidence.

We call the police officer's process 'critical thinking'. Solid evidence presents a logical explanation, allowing an experienced (or qualified) person to make a judgment call (or critical decision). It is the pathway of dominant thinking. Let's look closer at the scene …

The fire destroyed everything including surveillance cameras. Numerous fire trucks, police vehicles, and curious onlookers drawn by the smoke have made it impossible to find any tell-tale tire marks or footprints. The adjoining property's tenants/owners were absent, and the property doesn't have cameras. There seems to be no way to gather physical evidence. Should your investigation stop there? Maybe not.

Lateral thinkers free themselves from the shackles of dominant thinking. They engage their imaginations to search for new and original combinations that might reveal alternative pathways not immediately apparent. Before dismissing the investigation, you decide to employ a lateral thinking strategy of disruption— 'alternative perspective'.

The business owner's perspective: Imagine yourself 'pushed to the limit', losing money, and unable to cope. Your situation is so desperate that the only way forward is to escape the business completely. You might take out a large insurance policy. You'd remove cash and items of high personal value. You might even remove some of the stock and/or fixtures and fittings to sell later. Could the business owner have staged the whole thing?

You decide to investigate any insurance policies, talk to the accountant, search the business owner's home, and make enquiries into the 'health' of the business.

The landlord/property owner's perspective: Imagine your tenant being problematic and/or failing to pay the rent. You're behind in your finances because of the tenant despite knowing that the tenant has plenty of cash. He's undermining your investment and causing you stress. It's a long and difficult road to evict a tenant. You have plans to redevelop the property. The plans have been approved, or the council has rezoned your property, allowing you to modify your investment.

You decide to investigate any finance on the property, check with the council for any zone changes or plans for redevelopment, and determine if the rent is up to date.

The employee's perspective: Imagine yourself in a dead-end job, working for a boss you hate, earning less than you need to manage. You may have been recently turned down for a pay rise or had your hours reduced. Maybe you're facing repossession of your car or home. It would be simple enough to hide inside the premises at the end of the working day, open the safe at your leisure after hours, and then burn the premises to the ground to cover your tracks.

You decide to get the phone numbers of all employees and contractors to check if their phones recorded them in the area at the time and ask the business owner if he had any disgruntled employees past or present.

The firemen certainly had the tools on hand to break into the safe and make it look like a burglary. The adjoining property tenant certainly could have studied his neighbor's movements. The security patrol officer … you get the idea.

We're encouraged to think critically from an early age. If that were the only way to consider things, a lot of solvable crimes would go unsolved, and a lot of new and original opportunities would be missed. We'll be expanding our understanding of 'alternative perspective' in later exercises. For now, let's push forward and discover a powerful lateral thinking strategy that inspires creative thinking in others …

## Provocative operation, or 'PO'

A strategy to inspire new and original combinations from others.

> *'The factory is downstream of itself.'*

> \-    Dr. Edward de Bono

It doesn't make sense! However, the statement famously provoked some important and original environmental thinking—factories should always draw their water downstream from their own outputs. It's an awesome innovation that makes factories far more 'aware' of what they're releasing.

Welcome to 'PO'. Let's look at a real-life example to understand the concept better.

*Let's get naked!*

I was at a gathering of good friends in Melbourne. It had been awesome catching up with everyone, but the restaurant was closing too soon. Everyone seemed focused on saying goodnight. I didn't want the night to end, so I performed a 'provocative operation'. I stood up on a chair, unbuttoned my shirt, and shouted, "Let's get naked and go skinny-dipping in the river."

Yes, I really did say and do those things in the middle of a very cold Melbourne winter. So, what happened?

- It 'disrupted' the group's dominant thinking that the night was over, so that escape pathways (new and original combinations) could be revealed.
- Several people made excellent suggestions, none of which involved getting naked (thank goodness).
- Most of us partied on at a new venue.

*'Disruption'* is a term I'll be using frequently. It is a necessary 'part' of the lateral thinking process. The original suggestion of skinny-dipping in the middle of winter was a silly idea that was all about disrupting something I didn't like, to allow something new and/or original to be revealed.

*'Sometimes, lateral thinking is about taking a situation you aren't happy with ... and changing it.'*

Provocations can be nonsensical, funny, stupid, confronting, impractical, business-minded, or just plain daft. Oh, and they can be a lot of fun. If using this strategy in a business or professional environment, consider announcing your intention to 'disrupt' by calling out 'PO', or 'provocative operation', before you act.

The origins of the term 'PO' are disputed. Some claim it to be an extraction from words like 'hy(po)thesis', 'sup(po)se', or '(po)ssible', and was in use before the association with 'provocative operation'. Whatever. The point is that it's powerful, and it works.

I sense your fatigue. A short break ...


## Puzzle break - Their last dance

A couple enter a grand ballroom and discover that all the occupants are dead. There has been no crime committed. The couple are not concerned about their discovery. Can you imagine an explanation that makes sense?

Come up with at least one unique answer. If you're stuck, try using one or more of the lateral thinking strategies you've learned (random starting point, alternative perspective, or provocative operation) to 'disrupt' your dominant thinking. Some answers that immediately come to mind ...

- The couple is diving on a cruise ship that sank suddenly in a terrible storm.
- The couple own a pest control business and are inspecting the ballroom after fumigation.
- The occupants are ghosts, and the ballroom is set in the afterlife (in a fictional movie, play, or novel).

Feeling refreshed? Let's move on ...

## Backwards planning

Many of you will be aware that 'backwards planning' is an effective planning tool for achieving goals. It can also be used as a tool of disruption …

*Party time.*

In Australia, like many western cultures, we have a tradition called 'schoolies' (or 'spring break'/'senior sneak' I'm told they call it in the USA). Basically, at the conclusion of their senior school education, the kids take off to one of several iconic locations to celebrate for a solid week. Possibly the most popular 'Aussie' destination is the fabulous beaches and party atmosphere of Queensland's famous Gold Coast—a place where parents' nightmares begin.

Making things much worse in our family's circumstances, Julie (not her real name) and her seven best friends decided to drive (in two vehicles) the entire 1,701.9 kilometers so that they could 'enjoy the sights'. They had no plan, thinking that they would stop and camp 'wherever', and 'we'll worry about stuff when we get there'. Not on my watch!

I could've 'put my foot down' and argued long into the night, but I instead chose a lateral thinking strategy to disrupt their 'blinkered' thinking so that new and original combinations could be revealed. Their Gold Coast accommodation wouldn't be available until midday the following Saturday.

"Where will you spend Friday night?" I asked innocently. "So that you arrive fresh and ready to make the most of your time on the Gold Coast?"

The kids got online and decided that the scenic community of Coffs Harbour, just over a three-hour drive from the Gold Coast, was the perfect easy commute for the final leg of their journey.

"I'll get online and book you guys a camping spot close to the beach, shall I? My treat."

They backwards planned and prebooked the entire journey that included an exciting mix of sights, adventures, and destinations along the way, giving themselves an achievable three to five hours driving per day. As a result, all the parents felt a lot happier about the trip.

When you want to persuade someone, help them to imagine the ultimate outcome of their ambition, and then work backwards *with* them by imagining how they can achieve each stage so that escape (and potentially superior) alternatives can be revealed. Creative thinking can be inspired in others, even without them realizing what you're up to. Sure, argument and debate have their place, but sometimes the stakes are simply too high to argue.

I'll be delving deeper into backwards planning and refining your skills in later chapters. Next, let's rip up the competition's game plan, and learn to play with a different set of rules—your rules.

## Competition Vs differentiation

We learn to compete from an early age, and that's a good thing as it leads to efficiency, motivation, and success. Those that compete well are generally more successful than those that don't. As we learn to compete, we learn patterns that have been evolved over time by experts. We're evolving. But our greatest evolutionary leaps often come from those that aren't overly experienced or qualified and trying something completely different. They naturally differentiate because their views aren't 'blinkered'.

Experts are awesome at running your business, helping you to compete in that race, or creating something using the latest innovations and technology. They know the best existing practices and you would be foolish to turn your back on their wealth of knowledge. So, should we just step back and let the 'experts' do what they do best?

Experts tend to compete. Yes, that is the right strategy for a huge company wanting to maintain its leading market position or football team at the top of the ladder. But if you're not at the top of the ladder or just starting out in something new, you have an opportunity to differentiate, ignore and/or defy the experts, and not compete.

*'If your starting strategy is to compete with the experts, brace yourself for marginal results and/or failure.'*

Most experts will tell you the same thing, 'there is a best way of doing things and that's the way it should be done'. They 'know' this because of their expertise gathered through education and experience. So, what would happen if everything were decided only by experts?

- New ventures would struggle to find recognition.
- Competition would drive down profits.
- There would be less innovation and experimentation.
- Generic products/outcomes equate to less consumer choice and satisfaction.

Richard Douglas Fosbury won a gold medal at the 1968 Olympics by revolutionizing the sport of high jumping. Against the advice of 'experts', he jumped over the bar backwards. Elon Musk defied the 'experts' creating an entirely differentiated motor vehicle manufacturing company.

Here's some advice for the entrepreneurial/pioneer spirit starting out:

*'When you find that something special that you're passionate about, take the leap of faith. Trust your instincts and defy the experts.*

*'As you immerse yourself in your new venture, try not to become an expert. Instead, gain knowledge and experience only up to a point that you recognize and appreciate talent. Gather the experts under you and allow them to do what they do best. Experts will serve you well as the cogs of your machinery, and they are useful. However, it is you who must steer a differentiated course. Never allow the experts to automatically steer you on their proven pathway that competes.*

*'If you find yourself becoming bogged down as an expert, don't make the mistake of becoming a cog in the machinery. It's an opportunity to move on to your next passion.'*

Never be afraid to tackle something you know little or nothing about. Think of your lack of experience (such as not knowing the best existing combinations) as an advantage. Yes, there will be mistakes, setbacks, and failures. More than occasionally though, your lack of expertise will see your venture differentiate (find new and original combinations) rather than compete, and that differentiation is the path you should explore for *exceptional* outcomes.

So, what if you're already an expert, highly qualified, or experienced? Differentiation is still a choice that even the experts can make. The choice is made possible by releasing yourself, even if only momentarily, from the shackles of the patterns that limit your creativity (your blinkered thinking) so that alternative pathways can be explored.

Lateral thinking isn't *just* about problem-solving. It's also about turbocharging your ambitions, creating opportunities, and getting exceptional results. It achieves these outcomes by engaging our imaginations to explore new and original combinations—a process known as creative thinking. Let's keep moving …

## Teach as you learn

I wrote this book to combat the completely unnecessary complexity and confusion generated by existing lateral thinking literature. By now you should realize that 'lateral thinking is easy', and 'I can do this'. Let's make it even easier.

Demonstrating lateral thinking strategies to others is easy, fun, and productive. For most of you, the concepts seem simple enough, but implementing them effectively is an entirely different matter. It will take time and practice. So, practice as you demonstrate, and teach as you learn. When you teach, you surround yourself with like-minded creativity. As you teach, you practice your skills, expand upon them, refine them, and you build up your competence and confidence. You'll also be creating good habits of thinking behavior (developing neural pathways) that instinctively and reliably search for 'escape' pathways.

Start by sharing with someone close …

## Teach as you learn - Every character has a story to tell

Children tend to have their favorite bedtime stories that they love having read to them repeatedly. Through these stories, they're learning patterns of behavior, morals, and expectations. That's a good thing. It's also an opportunity to develop their natural creative thinking abilities. Let's start with 'alternative perspective'.

*Little Red Riding Hood.*

The wolf's perspective: Grandma was a bit 'tough and chewy'. I hope Red Riding Hood will be 'tender and tasty'.

Grandma's perspective: I hope the wolf gets my sickness and dies before Red Riding Hood arrives.

Red Riding Hood's perspective: Grandma sure has gotten ugly lately. I hope I don't look like that when I'm older.

Ha, ha, it's okay to have fun as you learn.

Briefly discuss each perspective to see if there are any creative thinking 'escape pathways' worth exploring (or conversations worth having). An example might be that Red Riding Hood was a target because of her youth. There are parallels there with reality. Another example might be that Red Riding Hood kept her thoughts about Grandma to herself to protect her feelings.

When older kids read a book (or write a book review for school), challenge their thinking by asking them to view the story through eyes other than the main protagonist. It leads to 'revealing' and 'worthwhile' creative conversations, and I can attest to the strategy getting exceptional grades for the teens in our home. The same applies to things like:

- Reviews in the workplace.
- A fundraiser strategy meeting at your local church.
- An argument over politics with friends.

Each experience is an opportunity to put your 'alternative perspective' skill on display, find new combinations, and teach as you interact.

We'll delve deeper into 'teach as you learn' in subsequent pages. However, don't wait until you've finished reading this book to begin. Engage with someone you genuinely care about. Maybe 'borrow' a friend's child. Or you could spend your lunch breaks practicing on a work colleague. Bring your partner into the picture. Find someone to share what you've learned. Practice one or more of the lateral thinking strategies *with* that person. You can also test them on the 'blinkered thinking join the boxes' puzzle, or try them out on a lateral thinking (situation) puzzle. And have fun!

It's time for a short situation puzzle break …

## Puzzle break - That sinking feeling

A boat is in a lot of trouble during a wild storm. One of the passengers goes below deck, finds an electric drill, and starts drilling holes into the bottom of the hull. The captain realizes what the passenger is up to and approves. Can you explain what's happening here?

My answer …

- The boat is a sailboat. The mast is caught up under a bridge. By letting in water, the boat will sit lower, allowing it to pass under the bridge and make its way to shore.

Try to come up with at least one 'credible' scenario before pushing on.

## Question existing patterns

In 'Teach as you learn', I spoke about developing good creative thinking habits, or neural pathways. The idea is that you should instinctively, reliably, and regularly explore for 'escape' pathways (new and original combinations). A simple discipline that helps to achieve this is to challenge existing patterns by frequently and consistently questioning 'Why?'

*'When we ask "Why?", we are often asking the more specific question … "Is this the only way to do something?" It is the easiest creative thinking 'good' habit I know.'*

Asking 'Why?' where the answer (or preconceived best alternative) is already known, is about breaking patterns. The 'disruption' will see your natural creative thinking ability come to life.

A real-life personal example …

*Travel routine.*

Why do I always drive the same route to visit my mom? 'It's the shortest and easiest route' is the preconceived best answer. I decided to occasionally explore different routes over the years. The results:

- Several new businesses (potential customers) opened that our company's sales representatives weren't aware of. I dropped in on one and brought in a substantial new customer. (Opportunity for profit).
- I spotted a local kitchen cabinet manufacturer/stone benchtop wholesaler I'd worked with previously who saved me about $5,000 on replacing my mom's kitchen compared to my previous preconceived best option. (Opportunity for savings).
- I saw a business sign bearing the name of a friend I'd lost contact with many years before. The friendship is renewed and thriving. (Opportunity for happiness).

Okay, so what happened here? I 'disrupted' preconceived thinking (the shortest route is best) so that new and original combinations could be revealed. Exploring 'escape' pathways really is that easy.

You'll note that in the above example, none of the new combinations have anything to do with finding a better route. There was a high degree of 'randomness', resulting in outcomes that were completely unexpected—a 'shotgun' disruption strategy. 'Why?' isn't necessarily so random though, it can also be a 'targeted' disruption as this next example demonstrates …

*To compete or differentiate.*

A small chain of auto wreckers invited our advertising agency to 'competitively pitch' for their business. The brief:

- Make their advertising and branding more effective against strong competition.
- Their target audience was males, heavily into motor racing and/or car restorations, who are extremely sensitive to price.

The 'normal' advertising agency procedure in these circumstances is to 'answer the brief'—to compete for the client's business.

> *'Competition reduces profits, so try to differentiate instead.'*

The wreckers spent an awful lot of money promoting themselves—sponsorships for car, bike, and truck racing, signage, auto magazines, and various other niche media. They tried to have a substantial or dominant presence in nearly every media typically frequented by their target audience. They were competing for a small market and making very little money.

"*Why* do you compete so heavily for such a limited market?" I asked them. The question stumped them.

Instead of 'answering the brief', we suggested they expand their marketing focus to a less competitive and broader target audience. We suggested a rebrand to a 'new parts alternative'. Retail showrooms were staffed by clean and professional staff in uniforms. Showrooms featured specials and restoration projects that could be delivered ready to start. Many parts came in new packaging, clearly labeled, with warranties on show. The retail shop prices were much higher than the self-service section out back that still competed with the opposition—a two tier service and pricing structure. Their advertising shifted to the broad audience of the state's largest readership newspaper. It was a huge success.

Our advertising agency often challenged preconceptions when pitching for new business. It was a strategy that didn't always win the business, but when we did win, we won it in a non-competitive environment which allowed us to charge handsomely for our services. Our profits were high, and so too were the profits of our differentiated clients—a truly 'win win' outcome.

## Are you keeping up?

Before we engage in some practice, here's a quick refresher of what we've covered so far:

- Creativity is about new and original combinations. Lateral thinking is about disrupting existing patterns to facilitate creative thinking.
- Through life we adopt/learn patterns that 'blinker' our capacity to 'see' escape pathways—our creative thinking diminishes. As more and more successful patterns surround us, there is less need to innovate.
- Think of lateral thinking as being much like humor. The 'answer' reveals an unexpected alternative that had always existed, if only we could have seen it.

- Expertise, education, and experience lead to competition. Differentiation is an opportunity for exceptional outcomes and profit.
- Disruption strategies revealed so far are **random starting points, alternative perspectives, provocative operations ('PO'), backwards planning**, and **question existing patterns**.
- Practice will improve and develop your skills. I recommend that you **teach as you learn**, surround yourself with like-minded creativity, and have fun doing it.

Okay, let's briefly practice each of the new 'disruptive' skills you've learned and see how they work together. It's also a great opportunity to start teaching by working through the example *with* someone …

(For more examples of lateral thinking in real-life action, please visit the 'Lateral thinking examples' pages on my author website: michaelmuxworthy.com. New examples will be added regularly.)

# Chapter Three – Build proficiency

## Practice exercise – A new small business venture

Imagine that you're helping me to set up an independent 'person with utility truck for hire' business to be run from my home. Things I might do include deliveries, rubbish runs, and small removals. I intend using online advertisements and social media to promote my services. Before starting this new business, let's engage in some creative thinking to see if we can enhance my opportunities for success and profit.

To get the thinking started, we'll employ some lateral thinking disruptive strategies. There's no 'right' or 'wrong' order of strategies. Let's start with …

My **random starting point,** a keyword chosen from a random book, page, and paragraph is 'river'. Let's explore how 'river' disrupts my preconceived thinking of how the business will operate:

- A river runs through my city that divides the population roughly into two. I could promote 'southside' and 'northside' special days to keep the jobs localized and efficient.
- Boats need towing. If I get a towbar, I could also offer towing or maybe get a trailer for larger loads.

Now you have a try. Choose a random starting point, imagine yourself helping me to set up this business, and see what comes.

The **alternative perspective** I'll imagine (or I could have asked her to contribute) is that of my partner:

- She won't be happy about me being on call seven days a week. Maybe there's an opportunity to give one of the kids a bit of extra work on weekends.
- She loves her social media. I'll bet she could do a better job of promoting my services than I could.
- Instead of an 'individual' business, she would want it to be a 'family' business where every family member has opportunity to get something out of it by managing media, taking on jobs, organizing bookings, or even managing my time.

Consider the alternative perspective of a type of customer (e.g., a local builder, small business owner, renovating homeowner, elderly person on their own, etc.). Imagine interacting with me on a job and try to determine a feature/characteristic of the service that is particularly advantageous/attractive for that customer. Try to come up with at least three 'things' that might differentiate my service before continuing.

The real **provocative operation** I performed for this exercise was with my two nephews. After briefly outlining the business proposal, I said to them, "I want you working for me." They weren't enthusiastic about the idea, but their responses opened some great creative thinking:

- "How much will you pay me?" Good question. My promotions should include a whole raft of labor options that can accompany the basic price for my service. Higher rates for two people, lower rates for a junior.
- "Do we really have to put up with working for you?" Hmphh! Well, no. The boys are welcome to source their own opportunities and I'll gladly assist them and let them use my vehicle. (They loved that idea, ha, ha.)

Come up with your own provocation and try it out on someone around you.

Let's now imagine the best possible outcome and then **backwards plan** how we got there …

My business is reliably and heavily booked at premium rates and offering opportunities for extra income to those that surround me if they want it. I have regular customers who value my service above my competitors. Before that?

- I have both a competitive advantage and a differentiated proposition that provides both steady rates of new enquiry and advantage for return bookings. Before that?
- My service and vehicle inclusions/capabilities are the result of thorough research.
- I've identified niche market opportunities.
- I surveyed potential regular customers for the sort of features that might be beneficial …

Try and come up with the next steps yourself.

Finally, let's **question the existing concept** and ask, 'Why am I starting a person with a utility truck for hire business?'

- Is this the best business to start? I should compare other business opportunities before committing myself.
- Could the business do/be other things? I could carry a toolchest and offer things like assembly and dismantling of furniture. I'm competent with tools in general, I could offer an additional handyman element to the service.
- Do I need myself in the business at all? I could start the business and subcontract the work out to other utility vehicle owners.

Come up with a couple yourself.

How easy was that? Make sure to engage with someone and run through the same exercise, but with an entirely different small business in mind— a child, your partner, a friend, a work colleague, or a roommate, and teach as you learn.

By now, you should be sensing foundational changes to your comprehension and perception of creative processes. You can lay those foundations securely and permanently through:

- Practice.
- Teach as you learn, and
- Surrounding yourself with like-minded creativity.

This is an opportunity to enrich your life *and* the lives of those you care about. Don't miss it.

Let's freshen up ...

## Puzzle break - Jealousy

Chloe is upset that her new boyfriend, Jake, has named his puppy 'Chloe'. She's jealous of the lavish loving attention she sees him giving the puppy. Jake, upon realizing the problem, covers a single piece of furniture. Problem solved. Can you find a credible explanation for what just happened here?

My answer ...

- Chloe is a dog but doesn't know it. She sees herself in the mirror and doesn't realize that *she* is the puppy she sees her 'boyfriend' patting. Something we humans do well, and our animal friends not so, is 'self-awareness'. The 'boyfriend' simply covered the mirror. Problem solved.

Try to come up with at least one 'credible' scenario before pushing on.

Okay, it's time to *really* ramp things up ...

## 'Exceptional' goal setting

This disruption strategy is life changing.

We all find comfort and ease in repeating the patterns that we know. We build career paths, hobbies, relationships, and habits that 'capture' us as we gain experience and expertise, and we become 'cogs in the machinery' of our individual circumstances. I'm not saying that's a bad thing. However, the 'disruption' of identifying our passions and/or ambitions (past and still unfulfilled, present, and/or potential future) is an opportunity to imagine how things might be different—an opportunity to explore 'escape' pathways for alternative combinations in life.

Virtually every single management and training course 'out there' will tell you to 'set achievable and realistic goals'. Today we ignore that advice. Today our goals have no limit. I invite you to witness my own personal journey *and* explore your own 'exceptional' goals along the way.

*'Imagination is everything. It is the preview of life's coming attractions.'*

- Albert Einstein

Einstein was right. Remember our creative thinking definition: *'Creative thinking is the ability to imagine existing things in new and original combinations.'*

Setting exceptional goals is about chasing your dreams—dreams that are fueled by your imagination. Creative thinking is the manifestations of our imagination. Lateral thinking is about making that possible. I often tell people …

*'Find something special in your life that drives you passionately and imagine where it could take you. When you're driven by passion, there are no limits. Your exceptional goals in life should revolve around your passions.'*

Let's begin …

**Step one – Identify something you are truly passionate about.**

My personal passion is developing my lateral thinking skills and sharing them with others. I attribute lateral thinking with my personal success and happiness, and it has helped me through adversity, illness, and some poor life choices, ha, ha. I regularly and passionately encourage those I care about to embrace the creativity made accessible by employing lateral thinking's disruptive strategies.

Your passion can be about anything at all. Some examples are:

- My partner is a passionate vegan who is 'driven' to create meals and food choices that tempt others to a vegan lifestyle choice.
- The child who won't stop singing along to the tunes on the radio.
- The entrepreneur determined to create a brand that survives them.
- Your past, but still unfulfilled, dreams of exploring the world.
- The parent driven to see a disabled child not only survive but thrive.
- The priest who works tirelessly to 'save' the local youth from …

You get the idea. Stop for a moment to consider, 'What's my passion?'

**Step two – Imagine the ultimate place your passion can take you.**

Personally, I dream of being a successful and world-famous lateral thinking author and protagonist. I dream of being a catalyst for change in a world being overrun by the groupthink mindset. I dream of having access to powerful and important people and influencing their thinking to unfold superior creative thinking outcomes. I dream of inspiring a generation not afraid to tackle anything. I dream of being remembered for my contributions long after I've left this world.

Ha, ha, it's not easy to admit that stuff out in the open. The truth is though, I really am passionate about lateral thinking, and I really do imagine those things. Now it's your turn. Take a moment to relax and imagine some of the awesome potential of your passion/s. There are no limits to the imagination, so 'go crazy'!

**Step three – Write down a goal clearly.**

The idea here is to write down something that can be quantified—that can be used to measure and/or judge your success. It can be your 'ultimate' goal, or it can be a substantial milestone goal towards your ultimate goal. Some goals, like my own, seem so far off that it's better not to plan that far ahead. Instead, write down a milestone that achieves much of the 'heavy lifting' of reaching your ultimate destination.

My personal milestone goal: Successfully launch an entirely differentiated 'awareness' strategy that takes lateral thinking to a much wider audience—'lateral thinking fiction'. Five million book sales is my measure of ultimate success.

Your turn. Don't be afraid, and don't worry about stuff like it being impractical or unlikely. That dream you just had. That 'thing' you just imagined. Extract a measurable goal and write it down in clear and unmistakable language. Right now.

**Step four – Tell everybody about your goal.**

More than just stating my goal here, I've published it on my personal website and social media, and I've discussed it at length with family, friends, successful authors, and several publishing professionals. So, how did that turn out?

- An 'expert' editor told me my goal was 'unrealistic'. Some even unkinder words were used also.
- A 'top' New York literary agent called my expectations 'delusional' for an unknown new author. True. (Ha, ha, I've been called worse.)
- Several successful traditionally published authors don't believe that lateral thinking has enough interest to sell that many books. They cited hurdles, and expectations, and blah, blah, blah.

The disparaging commentary from the 'experts' was expected, and only served to reinforce my resolve and confidence. Why? Because they are all 'experts', and as I've demonstrated repeatedly, 'experts' have 'blinkered' viewpoints. They cannot see 'escape' or 'alternative' pathways to success. They are 'shackled' to their own preconceived dominant thinking pathways. Potentially successful alternatives yet to be discovered will exist, and I *will* find one.

*'When the experts tell you that you won't succeed, wear it proudly like a badge of honor. All they're doing is confirming that they have their blinkers on, and that you've chosen to differentiate rather than compete.'*

Your turn. 'Oh no,' you think. 'I'm not ready.' I hear your doubts.

For your first-time use of this strategy, it's okay to build up your confidence by coming up with a goal from your passions that isn't too 'far-reaching'. As we move through subsequent topics, you'll be learning some powerful additional skills that we'll directly apply to advancing your goal. Your competence and confidence *will* grow.

Post your goal on social media, tell your family at dinner, stand up at work and tell everyone, or find some way to take the commitment well beyond your comfort zone. Take the 'leap of faith'. Do not be concerned by the seeming 'impossibility' of your task. Lateral thinking will smash through the blinkered thinking that has shackled you in the past.

**Step five – Backwards plan your goal.**

Many of you will have a preconceived mindset, or vision, of how to achieve your goal. Stop thinking forward. You're 'competing'. For now, ignore the competition, defy the experts, and dismiss existing pathways. My personal example of engaging my imagination to backwards plan my goal …

**Goal:** I've sold five million lateral thinking fiction books. How?

My research reveals that selling that many books through self-publishing isn't likely to happen. I'll need the distribution, marketing, and promotion resources of a large, international traditional publisher.

**Just before I reached my goal:** I secured a huge fiction book deal from a traditional publisher. How?

The major publishers require that you submit through a top literary agent.

**Before that:** I secured a top literary agent. How?

I spoke to a 'top' New York literary agent who advised me that I needed more than just a brilliant manuscript. I need prominence and recognition—some sort of 'edge' if I'm to achieve that sort of volume offer.

**Before that:** I'm a prominent lateral thinking protagonist. How?

My prominent, and highly optimized, multiple websites and social media platforms dominate the lateral thinking online landscape receiving many thousands of visits per day. I have several (five are planned, this is the first) self-published non-fiction books that dominate the available literature for lateral thinking enthusiasts. I'm regularly invited to do speaking engagements, training sessions, and appear in the media. I have an international network of lateral thinking 'players' able to assist me with my goal. I stand out among the 'clutter' of new fiction authors vying for the attention of literary agents. My lateral thinking fiction manuscript is judged to be 'brilliant'.

**Before that:** And the process continues …

Your turn. The backwards plan you eventually decide upon may take days, weeks, or even months to formulate depending on its complexity. By the time you finish reading this book, try to have at least one backwards plan roughly mapped out from end to beginning. Always plan backwards.

**Step six – Start at the beginning and move forward.**

Do not map out a rigid forward plan. The point of backwards planning is to identify a differentiated pathway. A 'vision' of the way forward is all you need. My example …

Most new fiction authors focus on their manuscripts, submit, and experience exceptionally high rates of rejection. Their dominant thinking sees them competing for limited opportunities. The personal 'escape' pathway I've revealed by setting an exceptional goal seeks to reduce the need to compete before I submit. Book deals come far more easily to those who have prominence and a strong online presence and customer base. The path seems clear … seems.

I must admit that there have already been numerous unexpected hurdles along my journey so far, and I've still got a long way to go. Things like improving my writing skills, learning about website development, overcoming the resistance of other lateral thinking protagonists with differing views, finding ways to broaden my target audience, finding the right editor, and many more. Like me, you will face unforeseen hurdles.

Think of yourself as being like an early pioneer traversing unexplored territory in the search for gold (instead of competing at an existing goldmine site). You have expectations about some of the obstacles you might face, but you can't anticipate everything. Do you stop and give up? No. You're equipped with tools, knowledge, and experience that will find a way to continue pushing forward. The lateral thinking tools, knowledge, and experience that you gain from these pages will see your drive and passion rewarded with new and original opportunities.

You'll note that I haven't mentioned a timeframe for my goal. There isn't one. All you need to understand is that if you keep pushing forward, you will eventually arrive somewhere. Sometimes, the destination might change as you see a 'mountain of silver' that diverts you from your intended 'search for gold'. That's okay. The longer you stay on the less traveled path, the more often differentiated opportunities will be revealed.

I've brought goal setting into the 'equation' early in these pages so that in subsequent pages you'll be able to relate the skills that you learn to tangible benefits and outcomes. For now, I hope you appreciate lateral thinking's opportunity to achieve exceptional outcomes that your 'blinkered thinking' previously considered beyond your reach.

A final point. Consider this to also be a 'teach as you learn' opportunity. Invite someone close to you to work with you in achieving your goal. Alternatively, help an employee, friend, or child set and achieve their own goals. Engage with others for an 'alternative perspective' to your goals, welcome their criticism, embrace their alternative thinking, but *never* surrender to their 'expertise'.

(I invite you to submit your own 'exceptional' goals for publication, and regularly update your progress, via my website: michaelmuxworthy.com)

## Teach as you learn – Random games, activities, & inputs

These are real-life examples of Random Starting Points applied to everyday situations. Work through them with someone close and see if you can brainstorm some random inputs into your normal routines.

### In the workplace – Random customer interaction.

An advertising agency I worked with had regular Monday morning 'W.I.P.' (Work In Progress) meetings to give focus and coordination to the staff's activities for the week. We'd talk about the demands of the week, deadlines, expectations, hopes, and priorities. We'd also highlight a random existing client for special attention. I cannot adequately describe the positive outcomes that resulted. Our clients felt special, and they were amazed at some of the innovations we'd put forward, usually finding synergy and efficiency within the week's existing workload and focus. That was a long time ago, but the experience was an epiphany, and it is the inspiration behind many of the random combination examples within these pages.

**At school – Random reading.**

A teacher I'm in contact with in the USA has a way to randomly assign reading assignments. Each student contributes one or more books they've read into a reading pool. They are then assigned a book from the pool that they haven't read. At the end of the exercise, the students talk about their reading experiences of both books and compare 'immediate' to 'lingering' impressions. They also discuss their experiences reading outside normal genres and/or interests. It's an awesome exercise to break reading patterns, broaden horizons, and explore 'escape' conversations.

**Younger children – The games of random things.**

Storytime with young children becomes 'interactive' when you let them choose their favorite story but try adding a random character (or input) into the mix such as a doll, toy, or character from another story. I added 'Kermit the Frog' and 'Miss Piggy' to a 'Cat In The Hat' adventure to finally discover where green ham comes from. A later addition of 'Henny Penny' offered explanation of where green eggs came from but saw Kermit in diabolical trouble with his beloved.

If I see a child (or young adult) engaging with a favorite toy or activity, I'm automatically thinking of random inputs that might enhance their experience and spark their creativity. I often combine random people in the workplace to spend time together helping each other out. It's not unusual for me to step out of my designated role and offer to assist someone who's job is completely unrelated to my own. I randomly sit with different people in the workplace for meals.

In group situations, ask each member of the group to add something random, and see how they might combine. I've done this at children's gatherings where I've combined activities completely unrelated for outrageously hilarious, memorable, and creative outcomes. I've been known to combine my clients in random circumstances that have resulted in unexpected collaborations and business ventures. I've combined random activities, projects, and holidays with my friends and family to build stronger ties and relationships.

Your task here is to engage with someone—anyone—and generate your own random input creative learning experience, and 'teach as you learn'.

Before moving on, let's freshen up ...

## Puzzle break – What happened to Betty?

When somebody unexpectedly comes across Betty by accident, without communicating, they immediately realize that she is lost, and they've solved a very old mystery. Can you imagine a credible explanation?

My answer ...

- Betty is a turtle with 'Please return Betty if found' and an address inscribed on her back. The address is in 'Siam', which hasn't existed since 1939.

Try to come up with at least one 'credible' scenario before pushing on, and don't forget you can submit your own lateral thinking puzzles for possible publication on my website: michaelmuxworthy.com.

## Teach as you learn - Backwards planning

*The tidy toybox game.*

We're about to break the shackles of a child's pre-existing mindset of 'it's a chore that I don't want to do', so that new and original combinations (for the child) reveal fun and desirable outcomes. How? By engaging the child's imagination using the disruption of planning backwards. Do each of these steps *with* the child …

**Step one.** Lie on the child's bed with the child and imagine it's the morning and you're waking up. It's a beautiful day that you can't wait to begin. Imagine your room being completely tidy. You leap out of bed and go straight to your toybox and open it. What is the toy that you most hope to find waiting for you more than any other toy? What is the next toy?

Have fun engaging with the child as they imagine the possibilities and the joy of a perfect start to their day with their toys exactly in the order they want them. Disrupt the child's preconceived notion that the toybox is a confusing mess only for the purpose of putting things out of the way to please Mom and/or Dad.

**Step two.** Next, imagine what happens before all the toys are put away. Close your eyes and imagine the toys all in a row, starting with the child's favorite, then next favorite, and so on. Imagine the fun of having to decide which toy takes priority over another.

**Step three.** Before the toys are lined up, you first need to gather the toys together. Imagine the fun of hunting for the toys, looking in strange places, and discovering hidden treasures (pieces of value). Nothing is left behind because for the joy to be realized, the toy must be complete. Imagine this. Close your eyes and describe the hunt for toys to each other, the strange and silly places you might look, and the important pieces to look for.

**Step four.** Okay, children have powerful imaginations. If you've got the ingredients right, you're ready to move forward. Let the hunt begin. After repeating the exercise a few times, the child will repeat this new successful pattern readily and enthusiastically with minimal supervision.

It's a powerful lesson for you also. Backwards planning is an opportunity to disrupt the thinking of others so that new and original (at least for the others) combinations can be revealed. It reduces arguments, changes perceptions, solves problems, and it can persuade people to your preferred viewpoint, method, or outcome.

(For more examples of lateral thinking activities that will inspire your child's creativity, please visit the 'Kids activities' page on my author website: michaelmuxworthy.com)

# Chapter Four – Expand your skills

## Creative combinations

*I can't do this on my own.*

My first position working in the advertising industry was 'New Business Account Manager' for a very large advertising agency. It didn't take long for me to realize that I'd taken on one of the toughest jobs in the industry—bringing in new business. There'd been a long line of failures before me. None of the staff took the time to get to know me as they assumed I wouldn't be there for long. Several weeks into the job, I was failing to live up to the expectations of my employment. Something needed to change.

The agency had a strict rule of 'creative staff are out of bounds', as every minute of their time had to be billed to a job 'in the system'. With nothing to lose, I began interacting with various staff to see if there might be some unidentified opportunities there. It turned out that a lot of people at the agency had a 'client wish list'—especially the creatives. The agency 'specialized' in a narrow band of focus that many of the staff found tedious and repetitive. They yearned for diversity, a challenge, and something they could tackle with passion.

Several staff started quietly feeding me 'tips' for business they wanted, sometimes providing me with clever concepts that 'opened doors'. It was the beginning of something— *combining* the wish lists of the staff with the problem of recruiting new business. I wasn't alone. I found myself with an enormous swell of support and new business opportunities coming from every corner of the agency. The strategy flourished.

So, what happened here? The original intention of the agency was that I bring in new business within their expectations (an existing pattern of new business guidelines). Working within the agency's guidelines wasn't succeeding, so I deliberately disrupted the pattern by seeking alternative perspectives from the creative staff, which lead to new and original combinations.

Let's quickly flash back to our definitions: *'Creative thinking is the ability to imagine existing things in new and original combinations,'*

and

*'Lateral thinking is a deliberate process of disrupting existing patterns so that new and original ways of combining things can be revealed.'*

We all have familiar combinations that we've evolved over time— patterns of behavior that work. We live within societal frameworks of existing patterns (work, school, hobbies, family etc.). When combining things, consider adding things 'into the mix' that you might not normally consider combining. Some examples:

- The university student struggling to maintain the balance of work, study, health, and a social life might seek employment in their field of studies, or invite their teachers and/or fellow students to participate in a team competitive sport, or they might combine study sessions with social activities. They could tutor lower grade students and promote through study-related social activities. They might even decide to only share accommodation with other students in the same field.

- A struggling parent might combine chores to learning, earning pocket money to workplace requirements, kids' sports activities to visits with the grandparents.

- A restless child will take renewed interest when you find creative ways to combine the things they love. A friend of mine's daughter absolutely 'flipped' with joy and enthusiasm when on a rainy day on the boat, we combined her dolls, her puppy, and the game of 'hide and seek'.

- The boss too busy to train might invite an employee to stick with them on certain days of valuable client interactions, or organize a ride to work together, or …

I'm sure you get the idea. Think about all the 'things' in your life that are 'compartmentalized' and have fun taking them out of their preconceived allotted places and combining them with 'things' you'd not normally consider combining with. Invite those around you to participate (teach as you learn) for even greater opportunity to reveal 'escape' pathways. I personally like to write a diverse mix of 'things' down on a whiteboard and then try to combine them in new, original, and often quite unusual ways. (N.B. 'People' can also be thought of as 'things').

*'Take the time to get to know people. It's amazing the combinations you'll find that lead to friendships, opportunities, problem solving, and much more. The more diverse your inputs are, the greater the opportunity for new and original combinations.'*

## Challenge dominant thinking

Should you challenge something that's already successful?

With many things in life, there's a dominant way of thinking, a prevailing pattern, or an accepted 'norm'. Often, it's because something is working, and 'if it ain't broke, don't fix it'. When you challenge something that works, you might face hostility, argument, and ridicule. You can end up alone in your cause, swimming against the strong current of existing opinion. Does that mean we should avoid challenging successful existing combinations? Definitely not. You can still explore escape thinking that 'goes *with* the flow'—tweak things a little.

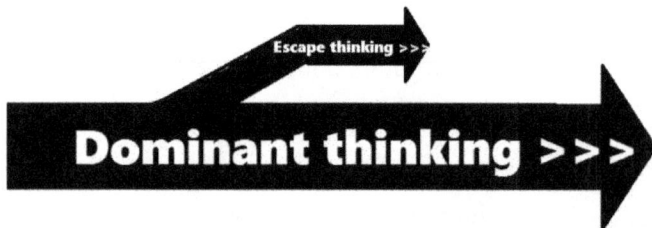

Imagine yourself in this situation …

*The school fair.*

Your child's school holds annual fairs after midyear exams to raise funds. The fairs are run by the local 'P & C' (parents and citizens organization) with the help of teachers and school administrators. The objective is to raise funds for school excursions. The fairs have always managed to hit their financial targets and much more.

Your investigations reveal that the school fair is a lot of fun. There are rides and competitions, locally made foods and treats, arts, crafts, and displays of learning such as science exhibits. The school and members of the P & C are rightly proud of their achievements. Due to its longstanding success, the fair has remained relatively unchanged for more than fifty years. Many of the P & C members have been personally involved for more than twenty years. Dominant thinking prevails with good reason, and because it is so successful, it's likely that 'challenges' to the operation are infrequent.

*'The accomplished lateral thinker questions everything.'*

Rather than try to drastically change the existing operation (a high-risk strategy), consider instead merely improving some element of the operation. When approaching large successful groups proposing to change what they've worked so hard to achieve, this is a relatively subtle and non-threatening review that *will* open doors and minds. Let's see what's in the mix (or can be added to the mix) that might be combined in new and original ways …

Teachers – students – parents – P & C – food – rides – classes – sports – learning – art – event management – security – marketing – sales – profit – insurance – tools – social media – community – recruitment – lessons.

I'm sure you can imagine a lot more things to put into the mix, but let's explore the above inputs for now. Some of the creative combinations that 'jumped' out at me:

- Combining major interschool sports meets on the same day/s of the fair to attract more attendance.
- Combine with an open school day to attract parents of prospective students.
- Let the students run/administer the event under supervision of the experts. Every aspect of administering the fair could be performed in classes—real-life learning.
- An opportunity to highlight the school's strengths to potential universities and employers.

My 'ultimate vision' is to further enhance the prospects of, and learning by, students through deeper engagement with the fair's operation overseen by the P & C's expertise. Every grade should be involved, with higher grades getting tasks requiring greater skill sets, and their accomplishments/inputs should be made evident to those attending. The existing combinations that have made the fair successful need not change. The enhancement is subtle, but worthwhile proposing.

Try to come up with half a dozen interesting combinations before reading on, and you could also try adding some new 'things' into the mix that are completely unrelated (e.g. the local vintage car club) for a more diverse range of possibilities. No matter how successful, popular, or dominant something is, there will always be alternatives, and more than occasionally, superior alternatives.

Think of lateral thinking proficiency as being like a tradesperson with a toolbelt—the right tools always on hand when you need them, and the skills to use them effectively no matter the situation. Let's test our skills and the versatility of our 'toolkit' …

## Public speaking

Here is an example of lateral thinking working *within* a successful existing pattern. This pattern 'disrupts' your preconceived mindset that talking to a large audience is something best left to the professionals. Lateral thinking enhances the outcome by finding new and original combinations (for the audience) that keep your talk original, authoritative, relative, and conversational.

**Four steps (successful existing pattern) to public speaking success**:

- **Step one.** Speak from personal experience.

- **Step two**. Engage your audience.

- **Step three.** Speak from the heart.

- **Step four.** Close with purpose.

I was terrified of addressing large audiences until I found the above formula. No matter what subject I'd speak on, there'd always be some 'know-it-all' who knew more about the topic (or thought they did) than me. When speaking from personal experience, however, I became the world's leading specialist on a topic. Nobody knows more than me about my personal experiences, my personal feelings at the time, or how an experience directly impacted me. It's a great formula.

The following example demonstrates lateral thinking's adaptability and immediacy, and ability to deliver creative thinking on demand consistently and reliably. Imagine yourself in this scene ...

*The alien probe.*

A huge and restless audience awaits the arrival of a specialized speaker on the subject of 'the psychological benefits of involving pets/animals in the rehabilitation of victims traumatized by alien medical probes'. The speaker is running ten minutes late, and you've been ordered by your boss to get up on the stage and speak to keep the crowd subdued. You know nothing about the subject of alien probes (hopefully). You have one minute to prepare. What do you do?

**Step one.** Speak from personal experience.

Speak with absolute authority. How? By using 'creative combinations'. Break the topic down into its smaller individual pieces and see how they might be combined in an original way (for the audience) that relates to a personal experience. The elements to potentially combine:

- Alien encounters? Nope.
- Medical probes? Hmmm, let's not go there.
- Psychological trauma? Yep, had my fair share of those.
- Support for the cause. Hmmm.
- Pets? Cats? Dogs?
- Animal experiences? Numerous.
- Healing? Numerous.

Okay, you've recalled a long-distant memory made possible by combining several of the elements and you leap enthusiastically up onto stage …

"Ladies and gentlemen, there was a time in my childhood when I faced a serious medical emergency. I felt all alone. I felt like my pet cat was my only friend, or so I imagined."

And you relate your personal experience about your empathetic pet and the trauma. By combining things from your personal experience, your words flow freely as they would in a conversation, and you speak with confidence.

**Step two**. Engage your audience.

Don't speak 'at' your audience, engage them with conversation. Help them to relate to their own experiences …

"Have you ever felt like nobody understands your pain?"

A possible strategy to employ here is to 'question existing patterns' …

"Why are we so emotionally attached to our pets?"

"How can a child that's loved by its parents feel so alone?"

"Why do we tend to overreact to injuries as children?"

The opinions and viewpoints you offer are based on your unique personal experiences and preferences and you are therefore the world's leading expert on the topics you cover. Things are going well.

**Step three.** Speak from the heart.

Whatever it is that you have to say, say it with passion!

"That cat saved me, or so I imagined at the time …"

There is nothing in your story that the audience can dispute.

**Step four.** Close with purpose.

Leave them satisfied by finishing with a clear point related to the original topic. If nothing comes easily to mind, go back to your list, and try new combinations …

"My mom put a bandage on my toe, kissed it better, and I was okay once again. I will never forget the love and comfort my cat gave me that day. It is the source of my passion for this great cause. Now I'd like to introduce our keynote speaker …"

It's okay to leave them laughing, ha, ha. Humor flows naturally when lateral thinking reveals unexpected 'escape' pathways (the completely unexpected combination of your sore toe, the cat, and your passion for the alien topic).

'Challenge dominant thinking', 'backwards planning', 'exceptional goal-setting', and 'public speaking', are all examples of lateral thinking co-existing with, or working within, successful existing patterns. Adherence to an existing pattern, even a compulsory pattern such as a workplace safety requirement, isn't necessarily stifling to creativity. Lateral thinking generates creative thinking 'on demand' in any situation.

As you become increasingly familiar with the various lateral thinking disruptive strategies, you will be able to engage them with the existing patterns that populate your world. Confidence and competence will come with practice and 'teach as you learn'.

Before diving deeper, I sense your need for a refresher …

## Puzzle break – Angry shark

A man dives for oysters for a living. One day, an angry and dangerous shark confronts him. The man has no way to defend himself, but he's not worried because today is his lucky day. Can you explain this?

My answer …

- The shark is a 'loan shark'. The man was lucky to have found a pearl while diving earlier that covered his debt to the loan shark.

Have a go, and try the puzzle out on someone close to you.

## Random starting points - Word association extension

This 'extension' to the Random Starting Points strategy can focus your results on a particular cause or problem—a less 'shotgun', and more 'targeted' approach.

Choose a random word (from a book, magazine, dictionary, etc.) and write it down. In a group or classroom type situation, write it where everybody can see it. Next, write down attributes or associations of the word that relate to the topic at hand. It's a very simple extension that we'll demonstrate in the following exercise …

## Practice exercise – The new marina

Imagine that you are a local government official and decision maker who must give the final 'green light' for the development of a new marina. All the appropriate plans have been approved, environmental impact studies performed, and required consultations with the local community undertaken. Everybody (dominant thinking) seems onboard with this project, and it seems to have no 'down sides'. Should you give your approval?

Hmmm, let's work through our disruptive strategies before making things final …

My **random starting point,** a keyword chosen randomly from the 'Angry shark' puzzle is 'defend'. Attributes/associations of 'defend' that potentially relate to 'marina' (our new RSP extension) include: wall – barrier – danger – prevail – protect – military – border protection – insurance, and try to add a few yourself before proceeding.

Okay, let's come up with some creative thinking around these new keywords:

- Is there an opportunity to secure the 'business' of border control and navy? A deep-water refueling station, or an assigned jetty to meet such needs might bring in regular traffic and income.
- The marina protects boats from the hostilities of the seas. Could it protect wildlife also? Protect people?
- Some natural habitats incorporated into the seawall could be investigated.
- Maybe an insurance company/broker could operate from the

marina.

Now you have a try. Choose a random (word) starting point, apply the extension, and see what creativity flows.

The **alternative perspective** I'll imagine is that of the owner of the restaurant I see as I look out from my balcony:

- Can I buy fresh seafood straight off the trawlers/fishing boats?
- Am I facing unexpected competition that might force me to close?
- Can food be delivered to the boats anchored at the marina? By boat?
- A boat taxi/delivery service.

Try coming up with more ideas from an alternative perspective of your choosing.

The real **provocative operation** I performed for this exercise was with a mate who owns a boat that resides in a marina. I said, "I'm moving you to a new marina". His responses were excellent:

- "Get in early to grab a position with easy access to ocean." (Should the local council be insisting it holds some key positions in return for approval? Police? Rescue? Fisheries? Border force?)
- "Will it cost more?" (Is the marina financially viable at competitive rates? Or is there adequate differentiation to secure premium prices?) There might be opportunities to differentiate not yet considered.

Come up with your own provocation and try it out on someone around you.

Let's now imagine the best possible outcome and **backwards plan** how we got there. For the purpose of this exercise, I'll backwards plan a single potential benefit of the proposal:

- The marina has become a busy gateway for tourists to visit a diverse portfolio of other local businesses and attractions. What happened immediately before that?
- Marina visitors were enticed by the region's marketing made known to them through their interest in the marina.
- Adequate provisions for marketing the region from the marina have been included in the proposal.
- A comprehensive marketing mix has been agreed upon.
- The greater region's tourism attractions have been briefed and given the opportunity to submit ... you get the idea.

Worth pursuing. Do you agree?

Now you have a go. Backwards plan this potential benefit:

- The marina is central to a massively successful rebranding of the region as a 'local fresh food mecca' that showcases the region's diverse agricultural products. Before that?
- The marina's marketing and branding (and name possibly) gives hints to the fantastic array of fresh food experiences. Try to come up with at least three more backwards steps before continuing.

Okay, let's keep moving. Let's **question the existing concept** and ask, "Why are they building a marina?"

- Could it be more than a marina?
- Is there adjacent land that might be developed with synergy?
- Would another location be better?

Come up with a few before proceeding.

Now let's try some **'creative combinations'** to inspire the creativity. I'm going to 'cast the net wide' here and include all sorts of local government considerations. The mix:

Road works – road safety – boats – fishing – food – aged care – schools – public transport – rubbish removal – wildlife conservation – crime control – health – property development – tourism – regional promotion – boat services. You should try to add a few to the list before combining.

Some combinations to get you started are:

- A safe place for the elderly to come and fish.
- An easily accessed rubbish collection point inside the marina for boats.
- Move the police station closer to the marina.

Keep going! Try to come up with at least five combinations of possible improvements.

Okay, now imagine that your boss is completely satisfied with the marina plans as they are without change. You might risk your job if you present anything that could cause 'unnecessary' delay. Still, let's **'challenge dominant thinking'** in a subtle way and see if any of our ideas could simply 'tweak' things for a better outcome:

- It would be a simple matter to explore the ratio of short versus long term marina berths after the approval and still optimize for the region's tourism benefit.
- A long-term plan for the immediate area around the marina could still be considered, even *after* the marina has been constructed.

I'm sure you get the idea, but come up with a few of your own, and consider some of the combinations revealed by previous strategies which might be subtle improvements that don't risk you losing your job or find you swimming against the strong current of enthusiasm to get the project rolling immediately.

Finally, take one minute to prepare for a five-minute **'public speaking'** assignment. Without notice, you are the opening speaker, addressing the local community at a town hall event. Remember, break the project down into the individual elements, and find a way to combine them in a way that relates to a personal experience (or imagine a personal experience of the official). For example ...

"Ladies and gentlemen, I'm reminded of a serious problem we had during last summer's storms. I got a call at ... blah, blah, blah ... which is why it is of utmost importance that we take this final opportunity to consult with the community *before* the marina opens. Please welcome our key speaker this evening ..."

Your turn:

- Write down a list of the elements to potentially combine and find something that relates to a personal experience of the imagined local government official and decision maker. (You'll have to imagine you are that person and his experiences, or use your own if you have anything that relates)

- Engage your audience.
- Speak from the heart.
- Close with a purpose related to the original topic.

Stand in front of a mirror, record your speech, or speak in front of an audience. You'll be surprised how easy it is to speak about a topic from the perspective of your own personal experience.

How easy was that? Not necessarily now, but make sure to engage with someone over the next few days and run through the exercise again, but with an entirely different project to approve from the perspective of a local government official. Practice with a child, your partner, a friend, or a roommate, and teach as you learn.

(You can find additional lateral thinking practice exercises on my website: michaelmuxworthy.com)

Let's move onto a powerful disruptive tool of leadership …

# Chapter Five – Take the lead

## Six thinking hats

I had the enormous privilege of participating in a six thinking hats exercise with the late, great lateral thinker himself, Dr. Edward de Bono. De Bono facilitated a high-level business meeting for a major Australian company for the purpose of exploring an identified opportunity. The meeting got fantastic results, however, the biggest 'takeaway' I got from the experience was the way de Bono so expertly and consistently kept bringing the focus back to where it was meant to be. He drove the group's productivity beyond anything I'd imagined possible from a four-hour meeting. It was a masterclass in leadership as he disrupted a group of very powerful business egos with 'blinkered' mindsets, engaged their creativity, and smashed through to a universally agreed upon vision and differentiated pathway forward.

Six thinking hats is versatile enough to use individually, with another person, or with any sized group you can imagine. I personally prefer using this strategy in business meeting or small group situations, especially where there are conflicting personalities/egos involved. It has never let me down.

Okay, the elements here are:

- A rigid pattern that disrupts—participants must 'wear' each of six hats that restrict (disrupt) their input to the specific focus required of each colored hat.
- An identified objective, project, problem, or opportunity to focus on.
- *Leadership* that must be adept and confident.

Let's get started …

**White hat.**

The white hat disruption always comes first. It is the hat of information, data, background, existing expert opinion, and 'what we know' (or 'what is'). Make sure the group is 'up to speed' on the agreed facts and foundations before proceeding. If any sort of data is missing, inadequate, or disputed at this stage, move forward by brainstorming what sort of sourcing and/or clarifications need to be actioned in the future.

**Red hat.**

The red hat disruption forces you to consider feelings and emotions— 'speaking from the heart'. 'I feel angry …', 'I'm nervous …', 'This is exciting …', or 'I'm relieved …' gives you some idea of the things your participants might say. Feelings and emotions, expressed openly, might surprise you. Never argue about how a person feels. Instead, try to understand the cause or source of their feelings. The opportunity to resolve doubts and/or negativity comes later.

**Yellow hat.**

The yellow hat disruption is about optimism and positivity. Imagine ultimate success. What does that look like? How do the others in your group view that success? What are the things that success brings? Only positive thoughts and contributions allowed. I sometimes create a prioritized list of positive contributions—an order of attack so to speak. De Bono grouped the positives into like-minded categories and formed a 'top three'. There's no 'right or wrong' way here. Find what works for you through practice. This is the most important hat of the exercise. Remember, your exceptional goals need not worry about preconceived limits. Use this opportunity to enrich the dream.

**Black hat.**

The black hat disruption is about caution, pessimism, risk, and negativity. You possibly sensed some of these attitudes during the red hat exercise. Build on that. Find faults. Face failure. Focus on the downside. Why? Because the best way to overcome adversity is to be prepared or bypass it all together. Forewarned is forearmed. If you can correctly identify problems (we'll be covering 'problem solving' soon), just like humor reveals an unexpected answer or response, lateral thinking will break the shackles that bind you to reveal escape pathways and solutions not yet apparent.

**Green hat.**

The green hat isn't necessarily about disruption. This is your group's opportunity to submit their ideas, and to contribute any expertise that might resolve problems, add value, and realize success. Remember, expertise is useful, but it shouldn't necessarily steer your course. Let the 'cogs in the machinery' contribute their expertise but maintain your differentiated focus.

**Blue hat.**

The blue hat is about process and control. When you wear the blue hat, you determine if all the steps have been followed correctly, summarized sufficiently, and that the key points have been properly registered. You may need to go back and further brainstorm various hat colors. You can also engage other disruptive strategies while wearing any of the hats.

In the middle of the blue hat process, De Bono asked the group to briefly don their red hats again and compare their 'feelings' to those expressed earlier that he had left written on a whiteboard. The changes in the feelings expressed were overwhelmingly positive.

The blue hat is also your opportunity to move forward. Canvas the group for their thoughts about what needs to be done because of the things you've identified. Set assignments. Designate responsibilities. Put the 'experts' to work. And make commitments—tangible commitments.

I cannot over-sell the power and performance of this strategy for taking control of a group and rallying them behind your chosen objective. It's a 'must keep' for your lateral thinking 'tool kit', even if it is only taken out on rare occasions.

This disruptive strategy is also an opportunity to advance your personal 'exceptional goal' and 'teach as you learn'. Work through the six hats with your goal in mind. Choose someone close to you to interact with.

Let's quickly freshen up ….

## Puzzle break – The helpful barman

A man walks into a bar and asks for a glass of water. The barman ducks behind the bar and emerges holding a gun. He then points the gun at the man and yells, "BANG!" The man leaves without drinking any water. Can you offer credible explanations as to what happened?

Possible answers …

- The barman had a long-running dispute with the man and wasn't in the mood to argue. His actions were a warning of what might happen if he were provoked. The man wisely decided to leave.
- The man had hiccups. The fright cured his hiccups without the need for water.

(Challenge! Create your own lateral thinking (situation) puzzle and submit for publication on my website: michaelmuxworthy.com)

## Quick review

A brief recap of what we've covered so far:

- Creativity is about combinations. Blinkered thinking (or a preconceived mindset) inhibits our capacity to reveal new and original combinations. Lateral thinking breaks the shackles of the things that inhibit our creativity.

- Expertise leads to competition. Lateral thinking differentiates.
- The disruption strategies we've covered are **random starting points** (with word association extension), **alternative perspective, provocative operation** ('PO'), **backwards planning, question existing patterns, creative combinations, challenge dominant thinking** (but go with the flow), and **six thinking hats.**
- Lateral thinking can work within rigid existing patterns to enhance outcomes, but also make use of rigid existing patterns as tools of disruption.
- Good creative thinking habits come from practice, **'teach as you learn'**, and surrounding yourself with like-minded creativity.

## Teach as you learn – Question existing patterns

Find an accomplice if possible—someone 'in on the game'. This can be a lot of fun as you 'teach as you learn'.

When I wrote this, I was on a boat with friends sailing towards South Stradbroke Island off the coast of Queensland, Australia. It is (or was) a favorite and regular destination. My accomplice is the nine-year-old daughter of the captain. We collaborated on the questions.

"Daddy, why are we sailing to 'Straddy'?"

"We always go to Stradbroke, darling. It's your favorite place."

"Why is it my favorite place?"

"Because it has sheltered anchorage, and it has easy access to the beach."

"Why do we need sheltered anchorage?"

"Because you get frightened in bad weather, darling."

My accomplice *was* frightened of bad weather at sea as a younger child—very frightened. Six years on though, she's very much got her 'sea legs', is quite adventurous, and feeling like a challenge (as we all were). We changed course to a more 'challenging' destination inspired by the many perspectives aboard. The pattern was forever broken.

A favorite place (for me) to 'play this game' is at the dinner table. 'What did you get up to today? Okay, why?' If performing this exercise in the workplace, it's advisable to let the recipient(s) of the questions know what you're up to.

Okay, it's your turn. Find an accomplice and identify an existing pattern to question. Perform the exercise with an unsuspecting audience and have fun exploring escape pathways. Use unexpected combinations, or even a provocative operation, to get the creativity started if nothing flows easily.

## Time management

I consider this to be the most important disruption strategy contained within these pages. Why? Because it makes everything else possible.

### 'Important versus urgent' time management model.

This existing powerful time management lifestyle pattern acts as a tool of disruption by shifting your focus over time from things that are urgent, to things that are important. I've 'married' the model with 'creative combinations' for superior outcomes that *will* free your time, enrich your life, and see your dreams realized.

Typically, most people manage time by making/imagining lists, prioritizing the things they need to do first, knock them off as best they can, and in what little time is left after that, if any, they choose to rest or recreate before the whole cycle inevitably begins again. There's not much time for fanciful stuff like chasing your dreams or imagining creative new combinations. Or is there?

Priorities and lists are the tools of 'experts' and middle management that live in the world of 'what is'—the 'cogs in the machinery' that are useful. More than useful, creative thinkers are exceptional. When you prioritize (or put into order) a list, you're effectively 'compartmentalizing' the elements and often imagining them as separate tasks and objectives. But do they *have* to be?

Consider these examples of how time spent on 'important' things reduces the demands on your future time and leads to superior outcomes:

- Quality time spent 'shaping' kids today saves an awful lot of drama and wasted time in the future.
- Exercise and/or a healthy diet today will reduce fatigue, days off, and health problems later in life.
- A quick 'scrape and rinse' of a dinner plate can save an awful lot of time scrubbing the next morning.
- Making the time to talk to an elderly relative about their finances, expectations, and preferences while they're able saves

you from a potential nightmare if they suddenly die, fall ill, or they are incapacitated in some way.

- Finding sufficient time to recruit the best and right person for a job pays dividends. 'Making do' with an underperforming employee will erode your future opportunities and time.

- Training someone properly today (kids, partner, employees, or suppliers) means the opportunity to delegate and 'let go' tomorrow.

If only we could find the time.

Let's create your first time-management model:

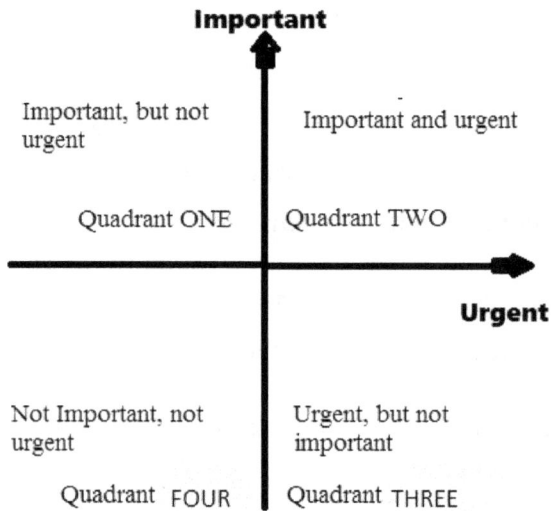

**Important**

|                          |                        |
|--------------------------|------------------------|
| Important, but not urgent | Important and urgent   |
| Quadrant ONE             | Quadrant TWO           |

**Urgent**

|                          |                        |
|--------------------------|------------------------|
| Not Important, not urgent | Urgent, but not important |
| Quadrant FOUR            | Quadrant THREE         |

Start by writing a list of your top five (only five right now for demonstration purposes) most important priorities in life. Put them in order of priority of overall importance, the highest to the top. Completely disregard 'urgency' at this stage, that comes later. An example might be:

1. The children's wellbeing (health, safety, education, and happiness).
2. Your exceptional goal.
3. Moving to a larger, more comfortable home.
4. Addressing your mom's accommodation and care needs.
5. Getting a promotion or pay rise.

Now take the same list and put them in order of urgency. For example:

1. Getting a promotion or pay rise.
2. Addressing your mom's accommodation and care needs.
3. The children's wellbeing (health, safety, education, and happiness).
4. Your exceptional goal.
5. Moving to a larger, more comfortable home.

(N.B. Think of 'important' as being the 'things' that would most greatly enhance your life, or the lives of those you care about. Think of 'urgent' as being 'things' that move up your list of priorities without necessary consideration of their 'importance').

With both list orders in mind, map out where they sit within the above model. The more **'important'** an activity, the further **north** it is positioned on the diagram. The more **'urgent'**, the further **east** the activity is positioned. Because these are your 'top five most important', they should all fall above the horizontal axis (quadrants ONE and TWO)—well above if you've identified them correctly.

Now, make a list of your top five most urgent priorities without regard for importance. For example:

1. Get to the supermarket to buy food for dinner tonight.
2. Paying the late electricity bill before the power gets turned off.
3. Attending a parent/teacher appointment.
4. Catching up on the rent.
5. Completing an overdue assignment at work.

Now take the same list and put them in order of importance. For example:

1. Paying the late electricity bill before the power gets turned off.
2. Completing an overdue assignment at work.
3. Attending a parent/teacher appointment.
4. Get to the supermarket to buy food for dinner tonight.
5. Catching up on the rent

Once again, map the tasks out on your model. They should only appear to the right of the vertical axis (quadrants TWO and THREE).

Finally, let's make a list of the top five time-related indulgences you allow yourself. These are things that currently occupy your time and energy but aren't necessarily urgent or important. We all need 'downtime'. It's an important part of your time management mix. Examples of things you might list here are:

1. Sitting down with your best friend after a hard day's work, relaxing with a drink, and discussing the day's events.
2. Binge watching a favorite Netflix series.
3. Playing golf.
4. Getting your nails done.
5. Going for a walk at the local beach or park.

Some of these will seem more urgent or important than others. Add them to the mix according to your own subjective considerations, but essentially, these items should appear in or close to quadrant FOUR if you've correctly assessed your urgent and important priorities.

Okay, have you created your own model? Great.

As your primary focus shifts *from* things that are urgent, *to* things that are important, the urgent demands for your time will diminish. Let's get back to our models:

- Quadrant ONE – **Important, but not urgent.** We typically spend far too little time in this quadrant, yet it has the highest long-term potential return for your time. Think **'dreams'**.
- Quadrant TWO – **Important and urgent.** We typically focus our efforts on this quadrant as it gives us immediate high returns on our time. Think **'must do'**.
- Quadrant THREE – **Urgent, but not important.** These are things that 'drain' our time, but they don't give us much of a return. Think **'poor return'**.
- Quadrant FOUR – **Not urgent and not important.** Indulgences and downtime. The things we like to do for enjoyment and relaxation. Think **'about me'**.

**Our objective**, and this might surprise you, is to reduce the time you spend in quadrants TWO and THREE, and instead spend your time in quadrants ONE and FOUR. That's right. Success and happiness, *and* the time to enjoy it.

**The disruption** here is that we've stopped compartmentalizing the activities that consume (or potentially consume) our time, and instead we're viewing activities from a 'bigger picture' perspective with emphasis on 'important', rather than 'urgent'.

**The modification** I've made is to employ 'creative combinations' to find efficiencies that make the shift of focus more easily achievable.

Let's work through the above example to see where some worthwhile changes can be made. Take all fifteen 'things' in the three lists and see how they might be combined creatively with emphasis on the 'things' appearing in quadrant ONE:

- Find a Netflix series to binge watch that also appeals to a troublesome teen.
- Share your exceptional goal with your best friend and make a point of spending a few minutes seeking an alternative perspective on developments when socializing.
- Teach the kids responsibility by getting them to pool their savings, go online, and pay the electricity bill or plead for an extension. (Of course, they'd be repaid, but …)
- Teach the kids (or your partner) to shop for, and cook, some favorite meals.
- The kids could earn their pocket money by doing chores or the shopping for your elderly parents.

How easy and powerful is that? The combinations become more diverse and more powerful as you add more things to potentially combine. Find some worthwhile combinations from your own model before continuing. Remember, focus on 'important', and wherever possible, 'important, not urgent' for the greatest possible paradigm shift in the efficient and effective use of your time.

**Abandon the model** once you've become proficient. That's right. Creating the 'physical' model is a short-term strategy only. Its purpose is to initiate good thinking habits of keeping the things that are 'important, not urgent' top of mind, and always looking for 'creative combinations' for efficiency and/or superior outcomes to facilitate that. If you feel yourself slipping back into 'urgent' territory, refresh your skills by creating a new physical model.

You can use this model to train others, or to derive outcomes within a family, group, or meeting situation. As you surround yourself with like-minded, time-management creativity, the benefits become exponential.

There is not a single 'urgent' demand for your time (existing, or future) that can't be alleviated, or eliminated completely, by changing your current focus from things that are urgent, to things that are important. When something 'urgent' does unexpectedly arise, you'll be in far better 'shape' to manage the situation without so many other pressing needs. You'll be surprised how quickly your urgent priorities get under control or fade away completely.

I suggest you reread this disruption strategy before proceeding, only this time create a more-complex model/mix of inputs that more comprehensively represent the greater demands of your time. Remember, the more 'things' there are to combine, the greater the potential for new and original creative thinking outcomes, and the more achievable your dreams become.

This really is the most important disruptive strategy within these pages.

## Puzzle break – Easily recognized

A man dies and goes to Heaven. When he gets there, everyone is completely naked and appears to be eighteen years old. He sees a couple and immediately recognizes them as Adam and Eve. How?

My answer …

- The man is Cain or Abel, and therefore recognizes his parents.

Take a moment to come up with an alternative and refresh before pushing on. (Clue - Why mention they're 'naked'?)

## Problem solving

This problem-solving pattern disrupts your focus from 'quick fix' and short-term solutions to determining the underlying causes of a problem and long-term solutions. The disruption invites 'creative combinations' for permanent and/or superior outcomes. It is a powerful tool that will help to overcome the many obstacles you'll face on the journey to achieving your exceptional goal/s.

Four questions to ask:

1. **What is the real problem?**
2. **What is the cause (or causes) of the problem?**
3. **What are the possible solutions?**
4. **What is the BEST possible solution?**

Let's look at a real-life problem I faced recently …

*Teen driving dilemma.*

Julie (not her real name) had just got her driver's license and wanted my permission to borrow the car after her mom had said 'NO!' Julie thought she was being treated unfairly.

*"If you hadn't made me finish school, I'd have a job and I could've bought my own car,"* Julie insisted. *"You would've had no say in it then."*

Julie and her mom were both in tears over the issue. They asked me to adjudicate—a truly 'no win' proposition. I declined, but offered to work through the problem *with* them to see if a solution could be agreed upon.

## What is the *real* problem?

Mom said the problem was about 'safety'.

Julie insisted the problem was about 'trust'.

*This is important!* If the parties to the problem can't agree, then you haven't identified the real problem.

After much discussion and more tears, we agreed that the *real* problem wasn't about safety, and it wasn't about trust. The *real* problem came when Julie's mom, concerned for her daughter's safety, wasn't convinced that Julie was ready for the difficult road conditions typical of our region. Julie needed to dispel her mom's fears.

(N.B. We've made no judgement here as to whether the safety fears are real, imagined, or reasonable. That is irrelevant to this step).

**What is the cause (or causes) of the problem?**

Mom cited:

- Beginner drivers are disproportionately killed on the road.
- The semi-rural roads where we live are an enormously different driving prospect than the busy and congested roads of Melbourne (a city of five million where most of Julie's friends reside).
- Julie's skills were not fully developed.
- Some of Julie's 'less than sensible' friends might encourage her to push beyond her ability.
- Icy roads resulting from gale-force Antarctic wind blasts hitting the region can be treacherous and unexpected.

Julie countered with:

- She's an adult now, and we should treat her as such as her friends' parents do.
- She would eventually have to drive on her own anyway.
- We've failed to take into consideration her exemplary history, and that she passed her driver's test without a single blemish.
- She'd done much more than the recommended hours of training.

I contributed:

- Julie should try to understand the sort of stress this causes us.

With a single clear problem to focus on, the tears stopped, and the rational contributions flowed.

## What are the possible solutions?

We got together, with Julie's younger sister also, to brainstorm solutions to the problem of 'Mom's (and mine also to be fair) fears not being satisfactorily dispelled by Julie'. These are the possible solutions we came up with:

- Do more hours of practice with me or Mom.
- Start with short and local journeys alone.
- No passengers in the car for the first few weeks.
- An advanced driving course.
- A journey computer in the car that records speeds/locations/etc.
- Daylight driving only for a while.
- Dry weather only and no icy roads until she's had specific driver training under those conditions.
- Being allowed to drive with a responsible licensed and experienced friend.
- Staged relaxations of the rules as she proves herself.
- Specific driver training on the busy Melbourne roads.

Okay, we have a 'gold mine' of things to potentially combine.

## What is the best solution to the problem?

This is why I'm so passionate about the benefits of lateral thinking disruptive strategies. We've disrupted the path of a bad situation, and we're about to turn it around into a positive. Here's the combination we agreed upon:

- Julie is allowed to use the car on her own for local short journeys only, and without passengers, until she completes an additional eight hours of driver training on the high-speed highways and busy Melbourne roads with an approved adult beside her.

- After the eight hours of extra training, Julie is allowed to drive to Melbourne in daylight hours, but no inclement weather, and no passengers. During this time, she must complete an additional four hours supervised nighttime training on Melbourne's city roads.

- That complete, Julie is allowed to borrow the car at any time that doesn't have inclement weather or icy roads. Still no friends in the car, though. Before being given open access to the car she must complete a further four hours of supervised training in poor and dangerous weather conditions.

- The vehicle's onboard computer, camera, and tracking technology must remain on.

Two weeks later, Julie had full access to the car. Her driving skills (and confidence) had improved considerably, and she was an inspiration of road safety responsibility for her soon-to-be-driving younger sister.

*'Where others see conflict, lateral thinkers see opportunity.'*

It's always a worry when new drivers first hit the roads, but I think we've given Julie her best chance of a safe motoring future.

(Submit your own problem-solving experiences that use this disruptive pattern for publication on the 'Lateral thinking examples' pages on my website: michaelmuxworthy.com)

# Chapter Six – The big picture

## Patterns that disrupt

We've identified six patterns that disrupt existing mindsets so that new and original combinations can be revealed:

- **Backwards planning** that reveals a differentiated/escape 'vision' forward.
- **'Exceptional' goal setting** that brings your dreams to life.
- **Public speaking** as an 'expert' by combining elements of the topic with your personal experiences.
- **Six hats** disrupts rigid mindsets by breaking down a topic into six specific differentiated considerations.
- **Time management** that's all about good creative thinking habits, focusing on the things that are 'important, not urgent' to free your time and create opportunity.

- **Problem solving** that disrupts by identifying the 'real' or underlying problem, and then generates things to combine for permanent and/or superior outcomes.

Throughout life, you will constantly have proven existing patterns (dominant thinking) thrown at you. Think of them as being tools for harnessing divergent energies behind your differentiated visions. **The proficient creative thinker considers successful patterns to be useful, but they are your servants, *never* your master.**

## Teach as you learn – The lost art of conversation

There is no better place to facilitate the process of surrounding yourself with like-minded creativity than the opportunity afforded when you 'break bread'. We've created an online digital alternate reality that seems all-consuming. It is the breeding ground of groupthink and indoctrination, and the antithesis of creative thinking. Mealtimes are one of the few breaks many of us take. Family, friends, or work colleagues, it doesn't matter who, make it one of your good creative thinking habits to disrupt the conversation at every meal you share, and explore. I do this habitually.

Lateral thinking's close relationship with humor will become evident when you skillfully disrupt blinkered mindsets, often with great hilarity, to reveal unexpected escape pathways that bring about enhanced outcomes and propel you towards your dreams. Over time, the recipients of your disruptions will witness the results, and they will appreciate and adopt the good thinking habits on display.

Choose a hat (six hats) to wear on a particular topic, say something ridiculous (provocative operation), ask a question where the answer seems obvious (question existing patterns), consider an unexpected perspective (alternate perspective), try tweaking a successful pattern (challenge dominant thinking), or simply choose something random to add to the conversation mix (random starting points). And never miss an opportunity.

## Pulling it all together

Lateral thinking is more than a bag of cheap 'tricks' or 'hacks' to be pulled out as required. The various disruptive strategies come together cohesively like an orchestra brought into harmony under the guidance of a masterful conductor. You are that conductor now. The 'harmony' is well documented in this real-life example ...

*Father/son patterns that interact.*

My good friend and past next-door neighbor, Dave (not his real name) had lost the very special bond he had with his ten-year-old son, Chris (not his real name). Unable to properly cope with separation from Chris's mom, Dave chose to keep his distance until 'things' had settled—a mistake as it turned out. Almost a year later, after civility between the parents had been substantially restored, the special bond with his son seemed broken. Chris had adopted new patterns in his life that didn't include his dad.

Chris's mom, who very much wanted Dave to be present in their son's life, confided to Dave that Chris *hated* having to spend alternate weekends away with his dad. He didn't like Dave's cheap inner-city rental accommodation, the 'strange man' that shared that accommodation, and he hated being away from his friends, toys, mom, pets, own bed, and comfortable family home on large acreage. Two overnight camping trips away with Dad had been reported back to Mom as 'a terrible time'. Chris had asked his mom to not force him to go on weekends away with his dad.

When Dave dropped in unexpectedly one day and revealed the problem to me, I suggested he set an 'exceptional' goal as a way to turn things around. Imagine you're on this journey with us …

**Six steps for Dave's exceptional goal.**

**One** – I asked Dave to identify something he was passionate about achieving in the relationship with his son.

Dave told me that as a family, they'd had many great 4WD/camping adventures exploring the Victorian bush (southeast mainland Australia). Chris had absolutely loved their adventures back then. Dave's passion was for the 4WD/camping adventures with his son to resume.

**Two** – I then asked Dave to imagine the *ultimate* place his passion could take him.

Dave dreamed of a future where Chris would be excited about their adventures in the bush. He dreamed of them planning ever more challenging places to explore as Chris grew older and gained skills and experience.

**Three** – The 'exceptional' goal (a substantial milestone goal in this case) Dave wrote down was for Chris to enthusiastically *want* to go on a camping adventure with his dad.

**Four** – Dave and I went next door and Dave openly told Chris's mom about his goal. She was very supportive and open to suggestions.

**Five** – Dave's backwards plan:

- Chris enthusiastically races out his front door at the sound of his dad arriving to take him away camping for the weekend. How would that be possible?
- Chris is anticipating an adventure that he wants to go on. Before that?
- Chris and Dave made plans together, including something special and/or exciting.
- Chris is open to considering time with his dad camping.
- Some sort of catalyst breaks Chris's rigid mindset (existing pattern). But what?

Okay, we've disrupted negative mindsets and identified a differentiated path to follow. Sure, there are gaps—big gaps. But lateral thinking *will* find solutions and create opportunities.

**Six** – Start at the beginning and move forward – Find the catalyst.

To begin the process, I suggested we list the things Dave 'wants' with his son:

- 4WDing.
- Camping.
- Fishing.
- Quality time together.
- A renewed and stronger father/son bond.

That done, we next listed the things in Chris's world that seemed most important to him. The idea here was to see how we might combine them in new and original ways (**creative combinations**). Some of the things we wrote down were:

- Chris's friends.
- Chris's ever-increasing desire for independence and privacy.
- Pets (dog and snake).
- Skate parks.
- Desire for a cubbyhouse.
- Comfort from familiarity of environment.

Okay, plenty to work with here.

The best combination came from Chris's mom who suggested that instead of dragging Chris away on alternate weekends, that Dave visit on those weekends (during the days only), using the opportunity to build Chris a dream cubbyhouse where he could spend time with his friends away from the gaze of his mom—an opportunity for father and son to bond. Not a bad combination, and definitely an opportunity to move things in a positive direction, but let's look further.

We invited Chris into the conversation for his **alternative perspective.** His enthusiasm was immediate, and the list of things to potentially combine grew:

- Sleepovers.
- A place for Pete (a pet python) to live outside the house.
- Wi-Fi and gaming.
- A fridge.
- Cubbyhouse located next to the pool.

If Chris and his friends were to sleep over in the cubbyhouse, it needed to remain inside the house or garage and within adult supervision— something that Chris didn't want. Also, Chris's pet snake 'Pete' was getting too large for comfort. Only about eight inches long when first rescued from local land clearing for a new housing estate, Pete was now over four feet long and growing rapidly thanks to constant over-feeding by boys with morbid curiosity about nature's cycle of life. Mom *insisted* it was time for Pete to be out of the house, reintroduced to the wild, and given the chance to find a mate.

We added the additional 'things' to our list of things to combine:

- Relocatable (or more than one) cubbyhouse.
- Sleepovers.
- Pete's reintroduction to the wild.

It didn't take long for a combination to be found that everyone seemed enthusiastic about. Dave and Chris would find a caravan that could be renovated into Chris's dream mobile cubbyhouse. The van could be relocated anywhere on the property and away from Mom's constant gaze except for sleepovers, during which time it would be moved into the home's lockable garage. The 'cubbyhouse' could be used for excursions away from home (familiarity).

The cubbyhouse had an important mission—the relocation of Pete. It's first excursion would be to the Dandenong Ranges, a highly desirable habitat for a python, where it would be used as a base as they explored the region for the best place to release Pete into the wild. Pete had become too accustomed to humans and needed to be located well away from potential future contact. Chris could invite his friends along for the adventure, and a last big feed for Pete. He was one very happy and excited boy.

We didn't work through all **six hats**, but we did put on the black hat to identify potential problems before they arose. Mom said that the van would need to be of a high and safe standard if Chris's mates were to be allowed to go along on adventures. She was also concerned about the boys sleeping in it overnight away from home. She wanted security lights, strong locks, and cameras. Dave was concerned that the lack of quality, high-speed internet access may be hard for Chris to accept (thank you Elon Musk for that solution).

Dave lived more than an hour away. Using the disruptive **time-management** pattern, Dave shifted his focus from 'urgent', to 'important', and found combinations that kept the project moving at full speed. Sure, there were problems accommodating Chris's expectations, but Dave was already an accomplished user of disruptive **problem-solving**.

When preexisting mindsets are disrupted and the 'blinkers' are removed, unexpected 'escape' pathways *will* reveal themselves. Dave's differentiated pathway didn't just find 'gold' or even 'a mountain of silver'. Chris's parents are back together and doing okay, something *nobody* expected.

> *'Creativity reliably enhances outcomes, sometimes in the most unexpected ways.'*

I like this example because it demonstrates the amazing harmony that's possible when the various strategies work together under the guidance of a skilled conductor. The differentiated pathway took less than two hours to be revealed from the time Dave turned up at my door—two hours! If it hadn't been, we still had a wealth of disruptive strategies in our toolkit ready to employ. Applying lateral thinking strategies for the purpose of achieving an 'exceptional' goal is the best creative thinking training and practice I know.

*'Never give up, just keep pushing forward with absolute confidence and passion knowing that for those that follow the differentiated path ... there are no limits, just possibilities.'*

Lateral thinking derived creativity *will* bring your life into harmony. As you develop good creative thinking habits (neural pathways), the individual strategies combine into a powerful and cohesive force for enhanced outcomes in any situation, and forever at your service.

Creative thinking is an amazing journey of exploration that is best shared. Surround yourself with like-minded creativity by ordering copies of this book for those you truly care about.

(For more examples of lateral thinking in action, or to submit your own examples of lateral thinking in use to be potentially displayed on my website, please visit: michaelmuxworthy.com)

## Puzzle break – Itchy trigger finger

A man pulls the trigger of a gun and realizes that, despite not shooting himself, he has likely killed himself anyway. Come up with at least three distinctly different explanations.

My answer …

- The small caliber pistol only served to aggravate the charging Rhino and focus its attention towards him.

N.B. Coming soon: Lateral thinking *fiction!*

*'We should NEVER have trusted the aliens'*

*Michael Muxworthy.*

A truly 'alien' perspective of our human destiny. Check out the 'blurb' on my website michaelmuxworthy.com/

# A final word

I attended a young child's birthday party recently. Typical of such occasions, I chose to interact with the kids rather than being drawn into conversation with the adults present. Something that I'll never grow tired of is the uninhibited creativity that naturally flows from young minds. *We* had enormous fun inventing crazy new games, creatively combining activities for hilarious results, and engaging imaginations to enhance the afternoon's schedule of events.

Late in the afternoon as things were winding up, one of the mothers who'd witnessed my interactions with children on several occasions, came up to me and asked, "How do you do it? How do you always manage to turn absolute chaos into such amazing experiences for the children?"

*'Chaos'?*

Animals instinctively play with their young. As they play, valuable patterns are imparted—hunting, competing, defending, even socializing. *Life is all about pattern recognition and development. It's how we survive and evolve.* 'Stay downwind or they'll detect your scent'. 'Those plants are poisonous', so we learn, and we teach our offspring to avoid them. 'Sneak up stealthily to catch your prey unprepared'. Before those patterns existed, they were unexplored pathways yet to be revealed. The challenges of survival necessitated that we innovate, adapt, and pass on successful patterns—survival of the fittest. Faced with imagined challenges of survival, children instinctively seek solutions. Their creativity thrives. Creative thinking is arguably the most important and valuable pattern we can impart.

Today, we're such a clever race, and we've developed so many successful patterns, that the *need* to individually innovate for our own personal survival is an unlikely prospect for most of us. We live comfortably and safely within existing successful patterns that provide and protect. As our struggle for survival diminishes, so too does our need for innovation. I sometimes think our society (as distinct from our technology) has stopped evolving completely. When I interact/play with children, introducing imagined challenges for survival necessitates their creative input. They seem to understand the purpose and importance almost instinctively. (BTW, I don't 'play' with *just* children, ha, ha.)

Chaos and randomness (unexpected challenges) introduced into play disrupts preconceived mindsets so that 'things' that the children accept as given (the preconceived mindset that we all get a piece of birthday cake) seems challenged (but only if we find a way to cross the crocodile infested waters, defeat the wicked witch that withholds the magic password, and overcome the villainous dragon that guards the cake). The children innovate and experiment to find solutions to the imagined challenges and dangers. To overcome obstacles blocking their path necessitates engaging disruptive strategies—seeking alternative perspectives, choosing random inputs, combining the things around them in new ways, and even challenging the rules, the game, and the gamemaster himself, are all encouraged. Creativity and innovation are ultimately rewarded with success, a sense of accomplishment, and sometimes cake.

*'If you were to design a universe to be everything it could be, central to that design would be chaos and randomness that forever finds new and original ways to combine things.'*

Lateral thinking disruptive interactions viewed from an outside perspective may seem chaotic and random, but in fact, they are entirely deliberate and by design. Things as important as our 'exceptional goals' in life are far too important to be left to chance.

Now that you have creative thinking firmly within your grasp, what will *you* design? You have no limits. It's *your* time to live *your* dreams.

\*

**Please, join the 'groupthink' fightback and spread the word …**

- Go online now and write an Amazon review.
- Practice your skills with someone you genuinely care about, teach as you learn, and surround yourself with like-minded creativity.
- Order copies for friends, family, and key employees.

# Glossary of terms and original definitions

**Alternative perspective** – A strategy of disruption that involves canvasing the perspectives of others, or, imagining (or role playing) perspectives other than your own.

**Backwards planning** – A planning tool that starts with your final objective, and then works backwards to see how you got there—a powerful tool for disrupting preexisting mindsets, patterns, and expectations.

**Blinkered thinking** – Where patterns of learned, established, or dominant thinking diminish or inhibit our capacity to 'see' alternatives.

**Cogs in the machinery** – Experts and middle management that live in the world of 'what is', or 'current best practice'. They are the tools that are useful for running things optimally, but their tendency is to prefer and repeat the patterns that they know—to compete rather than differentiate. Existing 'best practitioners'.

**Creative combinations** – The combining of 'things' in creative ways, often achieved by the combining of things that you wouldn't 'normally' consider combining.

**Creative thinking** – The ability to imagine existing things in new and original combinations.

**Creativity** – The combining of existing things in new and original ways.

**Dominant thinking** – A prevailing pattern recognized as being established, successful or a logical way forward.

**Existing patterns** – Ways of doing things, or thinking, that have evolved over time. They can be employed consciously through things like laws/rules, education/training, or social norms/expectations. They can also be employed unconsciously—things like habits, routines, and skills and strengths that you develop and rely upon. The 'blur' between conscious and unconscious increases over time as we gain expertise.

**Lateral thinking** – A deliberate process of disrupting existing patterns so that new and original ways of combining things can be revealed.

**Provocative operation** – A disruption strategy to inspire new and original combinations (usually) from others—an unexpected 'out-of-the-blue' action and/or statement that encourages creative responses/alternatives.

**Question existing patterns** – A disruption strategy of identifying, and then questioning, the patterns that populate our world—to question something even when the answer seems known or obvious.

**Random starting points** – A strategy of introducing something random as a starting point to elicit new and original thinking.

**Six thinking hats** – A tool of disruption that requires participants to 'wear' each of six hats that restrict their input to the specific focus required of each colored hat.

**Teach as you learn** – A strategy to amplify your creative opportunities by surrounding yourself with like-minded creativity.

# Notable Muxy quotes

Philosophical …

*'Life's great purpose is to evolve.*

*'It is our capacity for creativity that makes human evolution so exceptional.'*

-

*'If science and religion BOTH genuinely seek the truth, eventually they MUST agree.'*

-

*'If you were to design a universe to be everything it could be, central to that design would be chaos and randomness that forever finds new and original ways to combine things.'*

\*

The nature of disruptive creativity …

*'Sometimes, lateral thinking is about taking a situation you aren't happy with … and changing it.'*

-

*'The accomplished lateral thinker questions everything.'*

-

*'Where others see conflict, lateral thinkers see opportunity.'*

*'Creativity reliably enhances outcomes, sometimes in the most unexpected ways.'*

*'When we ask "Why?", we are often asking the more specific question ... "Is this the only way to do something?" It is the easiest creative thinking 'good' habit I know.'*

-

*'Take the time to get to know people. It's amazing the combinations you'll find that lead to friendships, opportunities, problem solving, and much more. The more diverse your inputs are, the greater the opportunity for new and original combinations.'*

-

*'Never give up, just keep pushing forward with absolute confidence and passion knowing that for those that follow the differentiated path ... there are no limits, just possibilities.'*

\*

For the entrepreneurial/pioneer spirit …

*'When the experts tell you that you won't succeed, wear it proudly like a badge of honor. All they're doing is confirming that they have their blinkers on, and that you've chosen to differentiate rather than compete.'*

-

*'Competition reduces profits, so try to differentiate instead.'*

*'If your starting strategy is to compete with the experts, brace yourself for marginal results and/or failure.'*

-

*'Find something special in your life that drives you passionately and imagine where it could take you. When you're driven by passion, there are no limits. Your exceptional goals in life should revolve around your passions.'*

-

*'When you find that something special that you're passionate about, take the leap of faith. Trust your instincts and defy the experts.*

*'As you immerse yourself in your new venture, try not to become an expert. Instead, gain knowledge and experience only up to a point that you recognize and appreciate talent. Gather the experts under you and allow them to do what they do best. Experts will serve you well as the cogs of your machinery, and they are useful. However, it is you who must steer a differentiated course. Never allow the experts to automatically steer you on their proven pathway that competes.*

*'If you find yourself becoming bogged down as an expert, don't make the mistake of becoming a cog in the machinery. It's an opportunity to move on to your next passion.'*

\*

Economics …

*'Let the market rule, but with a tempered safety net that reflects our evolved humanity.'*

\*

More books coming soon:

- Lateral thinking training – Train the trainer.
- Lateral thinking for parents, teachers, and educators – Grow your child's creativity.
- Lateral thinking leadership – Harnessing divergent energies.
- Lateral thinking for fun – Games, puzzles, and activities that stimulate creativity.
- Lateral thinking fiction – 'We should *NEVER* have trusted the aliens.'

Subscribe to my author blog at michaelmuxworthy.com for:

- book release updates,
- original new puzzles,
- a constant stream of challenging exercises and new real-life examples.

# MICHAEL MUXWORTHY

Michael (Muxy) Muxworthy has extensive experience in the fields of advertising, media, marketing, auction, and professional skills training. He is a strong and highly vocal proponent of laissez-faire economics—*'Let the market rule, but with a tempered safety net that reflects our evolved humanity'*.

Muxy's interests include exploring Australia's amazing coastline and beaches, sailing, snow skiing, techno music, and alien conspiracy theories (not necessarily in that order).

Muxy co-resides in Melbourne and Brisbane, Australia. He welcomes contact via his author website: michaelmuxworthy.com.